To Clive –

A hero in his own Time!

Bob

February, 1984

BEOWULF

BEOWULF

A Verse Translation with Treasures of the Ancient North

by

MARIJANE OSBORN

with an introduction by

Fred C. Robinson

UNIVERSITY OF CALIFORNIA PRESS
Berkeley   Los Angeles   London

in association with
Robert Springer   Pentangle Press

University of California Press
Berkeley and Los Angeles, California

University of California Press, Ltd.
London, England
Robert Springer / Pentangle Press
Marijane Osborn

Library of Congress Cataloging in Publication Data

Beowulf.   English.
Beowulf : a verse translation with treasures of the
ancient North.

I. Osborn, Marijane.   II. Title.
PR1583.08   1983   829´.3   82-16135
ISBN 0-520-04599-8

To Dave and Desi:
ic þæt eall gemon

Table of Contents

Acknowledgments

(Museum credits for the pictures are given in the section on "Place and Date of the Artifacts.")

It gives me enormous pleasure to be able to thank a number of people who have given me help and encouragement in my work on *Beowulf* in general and for this translation in particular. I am grateful to my husband, Robert, who has spent hours reading the poem aloud for me in his beautiful voice; to Gordon Stover and Elizabeth Dunlop for lending me their homes so that I could do research in their cities; to Fred C. Robinson (to whom I owe so very much), S. S. Hussey, Marie Ohlsen, and Gill Overing, for reading the draft of the translation and making valuable suggestions for its improvement; to the museum authorities abroad who have helped me to obtain pictures, and in particular to Ann Sandwall in Stockholm; to my tutor C. L. Wrenn at Oxford for his enthusiasm about my idea of using artifacts to illustrate the poem; to the Institute for Advanced Studies in the Humanities at Edinburgh University for making me a Fellow, and to the Faculty of Arts at the University of California at Los Angeles for making me a Visiting Scholar, both at crucial junctures; to Robert Springer who urged me to the task and his wife Nancy at whose elbow much of it was accomplished, for that and for shelter from the storm; and to my children, David and Desi, who have been supportive since the days they saw me through college, and to whom I dedicate this work.

Marijane Osborn
Reykjavik, 1980

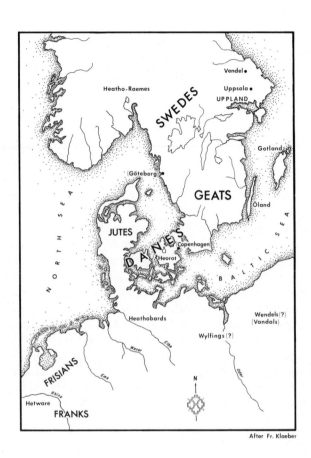

After Fr. Klaeber

An Introduction to BEOWULF

Beowulf is one of the relatively few major poems from the distant past which, upon first reading, still capture the attention of the modern reader and leave him changed when he puts the book down. Even those who have felt the narrative method to be flawed have usually responded to the poem's bracing severity, its awesome conflation of dignity and horror, and its strange, autumnal close. To an extent the poem transcends the slow revolutions in literary taste which have taken place since the eighth century: any modern reader can feel its moving power.

But readers require more from a serious poem than to be vaguely moved by it. The poet of *Beowulf* had a strategy and a purpose in moving readers, and to understand—rather than just feel—the poem the reader must have some sense of how the poet adjusted his medium to his narrative and his narrative to his purpose. At least three things are necessary for such an understanding. He must overcome the linguistic barrier of a form of English so archaic as to strike the modern reader as a foreign tongue. He must accustom his mind to a narrative method different from that of most literature read today, a narrative method which has little in common with that Classical poetic which underlies post-medieval European literatures. And finally, he must gain some insight into the thought-world of England in the Heroic Age.

The Language of BEOWULF

For readers of the present translation the barrier of language has been removed by Marijane Osborn. Wisely aware that translation is the art of taking as few losses as possible in a losing battle, Dr. Osborn tells us that she is surrendering density of language in order to give the reader easy access to the narrative. Her decision was the right one. The story itself is translatable, and the dignity of its telling can be suggested. But the morphemic richness, the artfully congested syntax, and the odd, continually resumptive movement of the original poetry would be intolerable to modern minds accustomed to having stories developed through lucid predications. A full and literal translation of the first sentence of the poem may help to illustrate the problem. The original Old English is as follows.

> Hwæt, we Gar-Dena   in geardagum,
> þeodcyninga   þrym gefrunon,
> hū ða æþelingas   ellen fremedon!

And the approximate sense in modern English is

> Lo! Of Spear-Danes in yore-days
> of nation-ruling scions of the family,
> —concerning their surging power our
> questions have been answered:
> how sons of landed nobility
>   fulfilled their competitive zeal then.

Add to this mish-mash the constraints of the elaborate Germanic metrical form, and we are lost in a poetic language so distractingly dense and self-conscious as to be beyond modern comprehension.

For the translator one of the most difficult features of Old English poetry is the pervasive phenomenon of syntactic juxtaposition. The sentences do not move from subject to verb to object. One element of the sentence is expressed and then, in mid-sentence, the poet stops to offer an alternative statement of the same element: "of Spear-Danes, of nation-rulers, we have heard the power, have heard how they fulfilled . . ." and so on. Not only the sentences, but the very words of the poetic language are constructed upon this principle of juxtaposition. The poet does not say "spear-bearing Danes" but poses instead the simple juxtaposition "Spear-Danes," leaving it to us to discover the relationship between the two elements, a relationship which is not always as simple as it would seem at first glance: Danes skillful with spears? Danes stalwart as a spear? Danes well-provided with spears? Because this fondness for suggestive juxtaposition permeates the Old English poetic method at every level (as we shall see below), it will be well to pause here to examine a few of the poetic compounds which test the translator's skill.

In line 159 the Old English word *deað* "death" and the word *scua* "shadow" are combined to produce *deaðscua*, a word referring to the monster Grendel. The full meaning of the compound is "a shadowy, death-dealing creature" or perhaps "a death-dealing creature who dwells in the shadows." Later (l. 703) Grendel is called *sceadugenga* "shadow-walker," an epithet with similar suggestiveness. In her translation Dr. Osborn is able to retain these compounds intact. But elsewhere such juxtapositions of words are too cryptic for modern English. In the Finnsburg episode the wounds on the bodies of the slain are called *bengeato* "wound-doors" (l. 1121), and Dr. Osborn translates "gashes" since no modern equivalent could encapsulate the intricate associations of the Old English word. For *bengeato* draws its significance from a complex of epithets in Beowulf and other Old English poetry which describe the human body as a house: *banhus* "house of bone," *feorhhus* "life's house," *gasthus* "house of the spirit," and *sawelhus* "house of the soul." The human body is a house of flesh and bone in which the spirit sojourns for an interval before its departure for the next world. Mortal wounds, therefore, are doors in this house through which the spirit escapes. The complex of these images develops a major subtheme in *Beowulf,* the theme of the sudden transience of man's life on earth. It would take an entire poem to develop the full sense of "wound-door" and "bone-house." And in "The Caged Skylark" Gerard Manley Hopkins produced such a poem after reinventing the compound "bone-house." Poems *in nuce* are precisely what these verbal juxtapositions are, and one of the translator's most difficult challenges is to resist their lure, to avoid clogging the narrative with hopeless attempts at reproducing juxtapositional effects which were natural to Old English but are alien to Modern. *Gleobeam* "glee-wood" must yield to the colorless "harp," *breostwylm* "breast-whelming" to

"emotion," and *hiorodrincas* "sword-drinks" to "loss of blood through sword-wounds." Our modern polyglot English with its streamlined structures of predication and modification can never achieve the effects of a highly stylized poetic diction deeply rooted in ancient Germanic habits of verbal juxtaposition.

That modern translators should not ape the diction of Old English was demonstrated conclusively by a disastrous rendering of *Beowulf* undertaken by the poet William Morris near the turn of the century. A passage like lines 280–81—

> gyf him edwenden æfre scolde
> bealuwa bisigu bōt eft cuman—

can only be rendered in something like the way Dr. Osborn has done it:

> —if change from this evil affliction
> can ever grant him relief again—

The unwitting hilarity of Morris's

> the business of bales, and the boot come again

(which seems to suggest wholesaling footwear rather than relieving affliction) is fatal to any passage, and such examples are common on nearly every page of his poem. And yet, one sympathizes with his effort to suggest those qualities of the poetry that are lost to the person who reads *Beowulf* in translation. A better way to achieve this end might be to indicate an approximate analogue of the Old English poetic method in a modern poem which succeeds (at least stylistically), and to urge the reader to keep that analogue in mind as he reads the smoothly paced rendering of Dr. Osborn. The closest one can come to the ancient forms in modern English verse, I believe, is the opening stanza of Hopkins' "The Wreck of the Deutschland":

> Thou mastering me
> God! giver of breath and bread;
> World's strand, sway of the sea;
> Lord of living and dead;
> Thou has bound bones and veins in me,
> fastened me flesh,
> And after it almost unmade, what with dread,

Thy doing: and dost thou touch me afresh?
Over again I feel thy finger and find thee.

The startling images, the juxtapositional syntax, and the exuberant verbal power of this stanza suggest something of the manner of the Old English longline at work. As a vehicle for a three-thousand line narrative this kind of verse would never do for a modern English reader. But for the Anglo-Saxon hearing *Beowulf* it worked splendidly, and the students of this translation should try to imagine for themselves something of the Anglo-Saxon's experience as they encounter the ancient story in its newest modern dress.

The Narrative Method in BEOWULF

A tactful translation can help the reader over linguistic and stylistic barriers, but it can do little to condition his mind to unfamiliar narrative devices. Without some preliminary attention to these the reader may mistake an unaccustomed literary strategy for a literary defect and may look in the wrong direction for poetic achievement. Following are some of the more prominent differences between ancient and modern narrative methods.

The poet's opening statement that "we have heard of the glory of the great folk-leaders, how those athelings did arduous deeds" should not be dismissed as merely a convention for getting the poem underway. The poet means what he says. His audience has already heard the tales he is about to tell. They know the figures of Germanic legend and what they did. This fact liberates the poet from any obligation to tell his story in exhaustive detail with who, what, when, where, and how spelled out at every point in chronological order. It enables him to be allusive, to give hints and gists of episodes outside his main plot line. Indeed, from this point until the end of the narrative the story of Beowulf unfolds amid rumors of heroism and tragedy from the Germanic Heroic Age. Sigemund the dragon slayer is mentioned briefly as the subject of the minstrel's song in honor of Beowulf's defeat of Grendel. The most renowned of all Germanic heroes, Sigemund is the subject of Scandinavian legends, and his story emerges again in the later Middle High German *Nibelungenlied*. The *Beowulf* poet expects us to recognize him and to see the aptness of the comparison of Sigemund with the victorious Beowulf. He also expects us to sense the tragic overtones in the minstrel's joyous reference to Sigemund's triumph over the dragon: Beowulf too shall slay a dragon, but unlike Sigemund he shall then die of the wounds the dragon inflicts upon him. Such foreshadowing is possible when the audience shares the poet's knowledge of his characters' fates. Later we hear of Hengest and Hnæf, two precursory defenders of the Danes, and we are reminded of the fabled King Offa, one

of several kings in the poem whose characterization provides us with a common model against which to measure the stature of Beowulf when he becomes king. Beowulf is contrasted with Heremod, a notorious tyrant who serves as a foil to the noble hero, just as the shadowy lady named Thryth serves as a foil to the good Queen Hygd. To the modern reader these allusions to names and events which are then dropped rather than developed can seem distracting or enigmatic. But in fact they are precisely in keeping with the stated terms of the poet's narrative. They provide his central characters with a context in a reverently remembered past, and that past lends poignant meaning to each contrast that the allusions offer.

Even those episodes that are presented in full rather than allusively may strike the modern reader as somewhat lacking in visual realization. We have come to expect in long narrative poems a wealth of description—the graphic details that Homer lavishes on his characters and their settings, the careful setting-of-the-scene in *Roland*, or the plethoric word-pictures in medieval romance. Of this there is little in *Beowulf*. We are never told what Beowulf or Hygelac or Grendel look like. The "high hall" Heorot is alluded to again and again but never really described. Scholars argue inconclusively over the topography of the poem, so vaguely does the poet suggest it. Instead of description the poet tells us the *effects* people and things have on those who encounter them. Beowulf is a man so impressive that a wary shore-guard is overawed by his appearance. Heorot attracts men from distant regions and casts its light over many lands. The haunted mere (which, in an exceptional set-piece, *is* described somewhat) is so frightening that the stag at bay yields up his life to the hunting dogs rather than take refuge there. Hrothgar seems moved to an impassioned exhortation by the ornamented sword-hilt he holds in his hand. (How different is the poet's brief account of the rune-carved sword-hilt from Homer's leisurely depiction of Achilles' shield!)

Almost systematically the poet ignores the superficies of things to dwell instead on their profound effects on those around them, and in doing so he reveals a set of mind characteristic of the Germanic culture he is portraying. In the dark time before Christianity arrived, the main positive good Germanic men found in life was the artifact of a life well lived—and the fame that follows such a life. A man or a thing enters memorial afterlife not because of appearances but because of effects. A man is remembered because he made friends love him and enemies fear him, a royal hall because it drew men from far around and touched their lives. In a culture where appearances pass away utterly while deeds are remembered, why should Beowulf's beard or Grendel's girth be measured? Anyone who reads the noble death speech of Beowulf and then complains that the location of his wounds and the expression on his face were insufficiently particularized has not yet understood the world-view of the Germanic Heroic Age.

The poet's proclivity for selective presentation and his emphasis on effects more than appearances lead to another unusual aspect of his poem—its narrative structure. A modern reader might feel that *Beowulf* has (as Johnson complained of *Samson Agonistes*) a beginning and an end but no middle. The first long section of the poem presents the youthful hero entering upon his first great exploit, the slaying of the Grendel kin. Then, at line 2,200, in no more than ten lines of verse the poet says, in effect, "and then fifty years passed," and we are suddenly plunged into the last day of the hero's life. The poet does tell us many of the hero's triumphant achievements during the intervening period, but these are all woven piecemeal into the many reminiscences and recollections that crowd upon Beowulf's memory as he marches toward his fatal encounter with the dragon. Structurally what the poet has done is to collapse end against beginning. Instead of allowing us to see his *Heldenleben* as a procession of events he forces us to view Beowulf's career as a stark juxtaposition of dawn and twilight, of hero's arrival and hero's departure. One effect of this narrative strategy is to direct our attention toward origins and destiny and to make us wonder whence the hero comes and whither he goes. That this is one intention of the poet is strongly suggested by the fact that we are introduced to this same structural pattern *in parvo* at the very beginning of *Beowulf*. The Prologue concerning Shield Shefing tells us how a troubled nation saw a young hero emerge from the unknown, grow to manhood and secure his subjects and then, full of years, depart across the waters toward an obscure destiny. The Prologue closes with the assertion that no one could say what his fate would be. The structure of *Beowulf* as a whole is in a way a restatement of that question, and the poem itself is a response—as the final section of this Introduction will seek to suggest.

Other explanations have been offered for the two-part structure of the poem, and no doubt there is some validity in them. Juxtaposing the hero's youth with the hero's age provides the poet with many opportunities for suggesting the pathos of human life, and the poet makes use of those opportunities with delicacy and restraint. The aged Hrothgar in the first part of the poem is a sad presage of what Beowulf will become; the youthful Wiglaf at the end is a poignant reminder of what Beowulf has been. The poet emphasizes these contrasts by shifting the epic formulas he had earlier attached to old Hrothgar to the aged Beowulf at the end and by shifting the formulas he had applied to the youthful Beowulf at the beginning to the youthful Wiglaf at the end. The result, of course, is to contrast as well as compare these figures: young Beowulf is greater than young Wiglaf, old Beowulf greater than old Hrothgar. Another effect of the two-part structure is to keep the essential moments in the hero's life before the reader's attention and to subordinate the less crucial events. And the essential moments are the moments of testing, the moments of ultimate stress. The youthful hero proving himself in his first great battle; the aged hero facing certain death—these are the moments that interest the poet. Anglo-Saxon poets are concerned to study man *in extremis* (compare the elegiac monologue *The Wanderer* or the great battle-poem *Maldon*), just as their Germanic cousins on the Continent were. How do good men comport themselves at the critical moment? This had always been a favorite theme. And no doubt there are other literary interests served by the poet's choice of a two-part structure over the more familiar (to modern readers) "beginning, middle, end." The latter is an Aristotelian, not a Germanic formulation, and, as Samuel Daniel has well said, "All our understandings are not to be built by the square of Greece and Italy." A close examination of Germanic "monuments of truth," adds Daniel, "argues well their worth and proves them not without judgment, though without Greek or Latin" (*Defense of Rhyme*).

In "The Language of *Beowulf*" (above) it was noticed that the root principle of Old English word-formation and syntax in the poetry was juxtaposition, and in the immediately foregoing paragraphs juxtaposition was seen to be the basic structural principle at the highest level of aesthetic organization in the poem. The conclusion seems inescapable that *significant juxtaposition* is a device that readers must watch for in reading Anglo-Saxon poetry. I believe this is true to a much greater degree than is usually recognized. Just as the poet constantly combined two independent words with independent meanings and then expected his audience to ponder their relationship and appreciate the *tertium quid* that emerges from their juxtaposition, so also he placed one episode alongside the other or one scene in juxtaposition to another and expected us to divine their mutual relationship. Perhaps the best advice one can give to a reader who has come to *Beowulf* for the first time is to urge a constant alertness to the significance of juxtapositions within the poem.

One striking example of significant juxtaposition in *Beowulf* is the most famous single passage in the poem—Hrothgar's account of the ghastly mere where Grendel's mother dwells. The ogress has just slain Hrothgar's favorite retainer in talion for Beowulf's killing of Grendel, and the old King hopes that the hero might be willing to undertake the forbidding challenge of tracking her to her lair and doing battle with her there. The account of the deadly tarn where she lives, with its almost unique use of descriptive detail, is usually cited as a "purple passage" in the poem:

> In a secret land
> they dwell, among wild fells, wolf-slopes,
> windy headlands where a waterfall
> hurtles down through the mist into darkness
> under the fells. Not far away

in miles lies hidden that lonely mere
overhung by trees covered in hoar-frost,
a deep-rooted wood that shadows the water.
They say every night there appears a strange
fire on the lake!—And no man lives
so wise as to know that water's depth.
Though the stag of the heath, pressed hard by
  hounds,
should make for the forest with his mighty
  antlers,
put to flight from afar, he will forfeit his life
on the shore rather than swim in that lake
to protect his head. Not a happy place!
There the wind stirs up sudden storms
where clashing waves ascend to the clouds
and the sky presses down, dark and smothering,
weeping from above.

Every reader of *Beowulf* has admired this scenic tour de force, but rarely does anyone ask why it is there. (E. B. Irving, in his sensitive *Reading of Beowulf*, pp. 76ff. does ask, and his comments merit close study.) That the King should tell Beowulf where the Grendel kin live is quite natural, but why should the poet be at pains to heighten the poetry so, making this passage so unforgettably evocative of the horrors that lie beyond Heorot? Thinking in terms of characterization, we might conjecture that the passage is there as a reflection of the king's desperation. His imagination has been captured by the horrors that face him, and in describing a landscape so sad and menacing that it seems to have a soul Hrothgar is in fact displaying the desolate landscape of his own mind. Although plausible, perhaps, this explanation does not seem wholly adequate to the occasion. It is more to the point, I believe, to notice that the speech of Hrothgar is one element in a collocation of two passages that form a dynamic juxtaposition. For immediately following the description of the tarn appears Beowulf's clearest enunciation of the heroic code of the North:

Grieve not, wise ruler! A man should rather
avenge his friend's murder than mourn him too much.
Death comes to all. Let him who is able
achieve in the world what he wants for himself
of fame and glory before he must die—
for the atheling, that is afterwards best!
Arise, great king, &c.

And the response to Beowulf's stirring speech is dramatic:

The gray-haired king leapt up, thanking God,
the mighty Sky-Lord, for what that man said.
Then a horse was bridled for Hrothgar,
a stallion with braided mane. In splendor
the king rode, &c.

What we have witnessed is a valiant young warrior regenerating a despondent king and his grieving nation with an affirmation of the heroic view of life. But the glory of the passage is the juxtaposition of Beowulf's words with the graphic horrors against which he is asserting his code. For the Anglo-Saxon audience, the real purple passage is Beowulf's vigorous articulation of the heroic principle. Or, better stated, the supreme moment in this scene is the point of juncture between the two speeches—that ignition point that releases the power and meaning of what is perhaps the most important single statement by Beowulf in the poem.

Another significant juxtaposition occurs early in the poem. Lines 64 to 81 describe the happy flowering of Hrothgar's reign. Men work in harmony to build the fair hall Heorot, and in harmony they occupy it, with king and court observing their mutual vows of love and loyalty. But harmony prevails only so long as men can repress the hatred, disloyalty, and violence to which human nature is prone. The dark impulses are introduced with startling suddenness in lines 82–85, and what follows immediately—almost as if triggered by the human violence just mentioned—is the introduction of Grendel. There is a suggestion that the evil spirit without is brought to life by the evil within. And we may even see in the juxtaposition a hint of the old truth that while men always imagine that the greatest threat to their security is the enemy attacking from without, in truth they are more threatened from within. And the narrative at large makes clear what the juxtaposition suggests: Grendel with all his horror made a nightmare of Heorot, yet he could not finally destroy it, thanks to the help of Beowulf. But Heorot *was* violently destroyed by a force against which Beowulf was powerless to defend it—the hatreds which lurked within the hearts of the Danes themselves.

Finally, consider the close of the Finnsburg lay (lines 1159ff.). After Beowulf's successful avenging of the Danes against Grendel, the royal minstrel sings of an earlier occasion when the Danes avenged themselves against an enemy—Hengest's destruction of Finn and return of Finn's widowed queen to her ancestral home in Denmark. The minstrel's account is joyous, but oddly the poet of *Beowulf* gives a melancholy emphasis to the story, repeatedly focusing our attention on the sorrows of the queen, who lost brother, son, husband, and her entire world in the violent encounter. Why this odd emphasis? The answer seems to lie in a juxtaposition artfully arranged at the close of the episode: "The lay was sung," says the poet, and almost immediately thereafter, "Then Wealhtheow came forth." The poet is calling our attention to an analogy between the two queens: like Hildeburh, Wealhtheow shall witness internecine warfare culminating in the burning of the royal hall Heorot. It appears from analogues outside the poem that the Danes were victorious in this warfare, as in the Finnsburg battle, but we are reminded by the poet's juxtaposition that victories do not end sorrows. The ill-starred Wealhtheow knows that the defeat of Grendel still leaves Heorot vulnerable to the envy and hatred in the hearts of men around her and seems almost to read the meaning of the poet's juxtaposing her entrance with the close of the Finnsburg lay, for she hastens to seek protection from the trouble she fears will arise from her ungrateful nephew. But her efforts will be unavailing. Dynastic struggles of tragic dimension lie ahead, and she, like Hildeburh, shall lose her dearest kin in the dispute. Here as elsewhere in the poem a simple juxtaposition of passages conveys presentiments of disaster which reverberate throughout the remainder of the narrative.

The Thought-World of the BEOWULF Poet

Beowulf is about many things, and the intellectual concerns that the poet shared with his milieu were no doubt numerous, complex, and beyond total recall. But it may be useful here to act out some of the more easily recognizable concerns of his culture, especially those which seem to have a bearing on his poem.

Many of these points of agreement between the poem and its cultural setting will be obvious. That a Christian poet writing only a century after his nation was converted from paganism should express pious views such as those in lines 180–88 will be a surprise to no one. That a poem describing the warrior class in the Heroic Age preceding that conversion should have little to say about the farmers and craftsmen upon whom any society depends will also seem normal to anyone who has ever read an epic or romance. But other attitudes in the poem can be understood only if we pause to consider the difference between our modern thought-world and that of the *Beowulf* poet. Consider the respective roles of nature on the one hand and man's artifice on the other. Anyone living after Rousseau and the English Romantic poets will be familiar with the view that man is born with a natural inclination toward wholesome conduct but that he is often corrupted by the artificial forms with which society surrounds him, such as inhibitions, social customs, and city life. To restore the soul we must return to Nature, for

> One impulse from a vernal wood
> Can teach you more of man,
> Of moral evil and of good,
> Than all the sages can.

No attitude could have been more alien to the pagan Germanic society depicted in *Beowulf* or to the early Christian society in which the *Beowulf* poet lived. Men in that day found no more comfort in nature per se than a thoughtful modern man finds in typhoons, black holes, or atomic fission today. Nature seemed anarchic, inimical, and life was endurable only in so far as man had imposed rational order upon it. The vernal woods were menacing, beset with fens and wolf-slopes, fires and storms, and uncontrolled, monstrous life. Against this aimless, teeming world man poses his rational craft. He strikes roads through the wilderness and dispells the natural darkness with lighted mead-halls. His ships conquer the turbulent wave and his ringmail and weapons keep sea-monsters at bay. Readers of *Beowulf* must be conscious of this attitude when they see throughout the poem the many references to cunningly made armor, artfully curved ships, damascened swords, and well-wrought buildings. Each artifact is a celebration of man's triumph over the hostile wilderness that surrounds the islands of order such as Heorot. The many artifacts pictured at intervals throughout the ensuing translation were not merely utilitarian objects: they were reassuring signs that man's rational order can be made to prevail over a formless and malignant nature. Perhaps the best visual emblem of this mind-set is the highly characteristic ornamental letter *W* from the Lindisfarne Gospels reproduced on p. 1 (in reality an inverted *M*). Such zoomorphic capitals appear at first glance to be abstract geometric designs— mere exercises in symmetry and balance. Closer inspection reveals that these designs are in fact highly stylized representations of beasts, birds, or fantastic monsters. For the Anglo-Saxon, the special pleasure in these designs was in seeing the bestial elements in nature constrained into meaningful symmetry. Out of two beasts the artist creates an ordered pattern; the pattern expresses a letter which is in turn a part of a word expressing human thought. For the *Beowulf* poet and his contemporaries this was the ideal relationship between man and nature.

Nor is the *Beowulf* poet's delight in rationalizing nature limited to external nature. Human nature, when it escapes man's control, is perhaps the most dangerous force of all, as some of the preceding discussion has suggested. We find much in *Beowulf*, therefore, about the forms and customs by which men ordered their lives. Greetings, speeches, preparations for battle are performed almost ritualistically. The herald who takes Beowulf's message to King Hrothgar does so standing "before his shoulder, according to the nobel custom." All this is not mere *mise en scène*; it expresses a major theme in the poem, reminding us that men must ever strive for control, not yield to impulse. The same is true of the mead-serving ceremony and the formalities of seating guests and taking food. We never hear of feasts without ceremony—except when Grendel falls to his gruesome repast, or when the evil Heremod explodes with anger and slays his table companions. To the *Beowulf* poet such conduct as this is not human. It is natural.

The characters in *Beowulf* and the poet himself do not shrink from moral judgments. A man who slays his own kin is treacherous, not (as such a man might be judged today) in need of psychological counseling. A man who deserts his comrades in battle is a coward, not a respectable dissenter marching to a different drummer. A ruler who usurps the wealth that is owed to his followers is condemned and expelled; he is not, like some modern embezzlers, excused on the grounds that he was working under an emotional strain. A king whom old age has crippled may be excused as blameless even though he can no longer protect his people; but otherwise one is held responsible for his actions. Some modern critics have resisted this stern strain in the Anglo-Saxon outlook. They believe Beowulf's heroic stature is qualified by the poet, and the monsters, though evil, have something to be said in their defense. Such views smack of the modern world, not of the world of *Beowulf*.

And yet, moral judgments in the poem are not merely simplistic. In a sense, the entire narrative is a subtle questioning of the prevailing (eighth-century) moral judgment of the Heroic Age. But to understand this we must examine one further aspect of the thought-world of *Beowulf*, the confrontation of Christian and pagan beliefs in Dark Age England.

The standard Christian authorities in the time of the *Beowulf* poet left no room for uncertainty in assessing the confrontation of Christian and pagan: Christianity was the Truth and paganism was a treacherous network of lies and deceptions fabricated by the Devil. Any devout Christian, including the *Beowulf* poet, would presumably have accepted this view without question. A logical corollary to this view which Christians would also have been expected to accept, is the dictum expressed most clearly by St. Cyprian: "There is no salvation outside the Church." Most Anglo-Saxons who wrote on this subject espoused Cyprian's view without difficulty, but for some the implications were troubling. For to accept this view meant that one was willing to see one's ancestors consigned to eternal damnation. To kings who traced their lineage back to Woden and aristocrats who took pride in the works and wisdom of their Continental forebears, the consequences of accepting the Christian view could involve some pain. Many,

no doubt, tried not to dwell on the past, turning their minds instead toward the Christian present and future.

And yet it is precisely this condemned ancestry of the English to which the *Beowulf* poet has devoted his poem. Though himself a Christian, and probably the son and grandson of Christians, he does not write of the Christian heroes celebrated by many of his fellow poets but turns his gaze back to the Continent in the fifth and sixth centuries, back to his ancestors in the dark and hopeless past. He knows of their desperate situation in the Christian scheme of things, for he refers to the heathen practices of his characters (lines 175ff.):

> At times they vowed in idol-tents
> to sacrifice, &c.

and to the consequences of their heathenism:

> Woe be to him
> who because of strife must shove his soul
> to the heart of the fire! He cannot hope
> for help or change, ever.

But having acknowledged that his heroes lived in the days of heathen ignorance and having recognized the consequences of their benighted condition, he proceeds to tell their story with the deepest respect, admiring their generosity, praising their dignity, and exalting their prowess, right up to the moment that Beowulf departs this life.

Such treatment of his subject by the *Beowulf* poet was in a way daring, for churchmen in his day (and before) were emphatic in their declarations that pagan ancestors should not only be consigned to damnation but that they should also be forgotten. In his letter to the monks of Lindisfarne the eighth-century cleric Alcuin states the matter clearly when he exhorts the brothers to stop listening to stories of pagan heroes like Ingeld:

> Let the words of God be read at the meal of the clergy. There it is fitting to hear the lector, not a harp-player; the sermons of the Fathers, not songs of heathens. For what has Ingeld to do with Christ? Narrow is the house; it cannot hold both. The King of Heaven will have nothing to do with so-called kings who are heathen and damned. For the One King rules eternally in Heaven, while the heathen is damned and howls in hell.

Is it impermissible, then, even to acknowledge that heathens were capable of good acts? Tertullian had an answer: "The virtues of the heathen, being devoid of grace, can only be looked upon as splendid vices" *(De Carne Christi).*

Not every voice concurred in this harsh judgment. Anglo-Saxon missionaries on the Continent in the eighth century reported to their countrymen that the conduct of Germanic heathens was sometimes admirable, even though they were deprived of Christian revelation. In the neighboring Celtic regions Christian thinkers wondered whether truly virtuous men might not find salvation outside the Church if they intuitively sensed God's precepts and followed them. But these were minority voices, and the poet of *Beowulf* does not invoke their doctrines, if he knew them. Rather, through literary strategies he seeks to make a place for the noble ancestors in the memory of his nation. On the one hand he is forthright in acknowledging that Beowulf and his contemporaries were pagans. The speech Beowulf makes to Hrothgar following the description of Grendel's mere is from the pagan Germanic world and could never be reconciled to Christianity. The omens the Geats seek to read by casting lots (lines 204–5), the totemic animals that protect their armor, and the allusions to Weland and Wyrd are all elements of pagan Germanic culture. And at his death Beowulf is cremated (an abomination to eighth-century Christians) and the tumulus reared over his remains seems almost a heroön, so reverent are the praises that his comrades chant to his memory.

And yet, along with these pagan details in Beowulf's characterization, the poet has in other respects portrayed his hero as a man of such virtue as to suggest, at times, the example of Christ Himself. Beowulf's entire career is one of self-sacrifice, as he repeatedly risks (and ultimately gives) his life for the salvation and protection of his people. While not a Christian, Beowulf is nonetheless deeply religious, for although he never refers to Christ or to anything pertaining to the Church, he does refer often to an all-powerful Higher Being which rules the world and men's actions. He thanks this Being for his triumphs, he ascribes his strength to Him, and near the end of the poem he worries over the possibility of his having offended this Higher Being in some way of which he is unaware. He attains to virtue by adhering to the tenets of the old Germanic code, but he does so with such piety that he seems to approach the Christian ideal. His kindness is revealed when he refuses to accept the throne which Hygd offers him, preferring out of Germanic loyalty and love to help a young, weaker man to rule. At his death, Beowulf never condemns the cowardly retainers who deserted him in his hour of need; his thoughts are always and exclusively on the survival of his people. In their conception of nature (as was discussed above) and in many other things the pagan and the Christian views converged, and the poet emphasizes these points of convergence.

The poet's most imaginative device for portraying the pagan Beowulf as deserving of an honorable place in the Christian thought-world is in his conception of evil in the poem. It is in the monsters, as J. R. R. Tolkien has pointed out, that we find an objective realization of all that is evil in heroic life and, at the same time, the center of evil in the Christian view. The accommodation of the two is clearest in the poet's tracing of the genealogy of Grendel in lines 105–14 (and again in lines 1261ff.). He tells us that Grendel is the descendant of Cain, thus giving him Judaeo-Christian ancestry. But the line of descent includes giants and elves and walking dead—creatures that have no place in Biblical lore but rather are from the demonology of the pagan Germanic peoples. These creatures, according to Northern mythology, were the enemies of gods and men, the forces of chaos and brute violence seeking always to undo the order that good men and good gods have brought to the world. Grendel and his mother (and later the dragon) are embodiments of the evil force as it was conceived by Christians and, simultaneously, of the evil side of the Germanic heroic life.

By pitting the hero Beowulf against the monsters thus defined, the poet has his hero join forces, unwittingly, with the Christian Anglo-Saxons of later years. This enables Christian Anglo-Saxons to identify positively with their pagan forefathers and thus retain pride of ancestry despite the theological gulf that divides them: Beowulf, though ignorant of Christian revelation, is nonetheless fighting against the same enemy that Christians of the poet's own day are fighting. While we can understand the Good only through Revelation and conversion, Evil is always the same. Cruelty and violence, whether manifested in Heremod or Cain, in the dragon of the Apocalypse or the dragon of Germanic mythology, are peculiar to no creed or culture. With this sad truth the poet of *Beowulf* was able to establish a place for the noble pagan in the collective memory of Christian Anglo-Saxons.

The *Beowulf* poet is not the first to build with poetry a place for his nation's past, but he has done it in a manner that is uniquely moving. There is an air of mystery and pathos in *Beowulf* that readers rarely forget. In part this is because the question of Beowulf's destiny beyond life is never clearly resolved. "His soul went forth," the poet says, "to seek the judgment of the just." The vagueness is deliberate, for the stern voices of early Christian dogma cannot be imagined away. Perhaps we must regard all the virtues of Beowulf as nothing more than "splendid vices"; perhaps the only just judgment for him after his pagan funeral *is* damnation. No word in the poem denies this. But the poet's tone—a tone of unqualified admiration for the hero maintained throughout three thousand lines of poetry—protests against such a judgment. We are thus left at the end of *Beowulf* with a delicately poised contradiction and a sad uncertainty. It is an uncertainty which for many centuries has darkened men's broodings over life and afterlife.

A modern example of such brooding provides an illuminating analogue to the conflicting feelings with which the poet closes *Beowulf*. The twentieth-century Spanish thinker Miguel de Unamuno engaged the subject of life after death in a moving philosophical meditation called "Del sentimiento trágico de la vida" ("On the Tragic Sense of Life"). After several agonized chapters on man's need for a belief in personal immortality, Unamuno finally acknowledges that there may after all be no afterlife, and hence no meaning in human existence. This terrible realization urges the author to the finest sentence in this book: "Y si es la nada lo que nos está reservado, hagamos que sea una injusticia esto!" ("And if it is oblivion that is reserved for us at the end of this life, then let us act in such a way that this will have been an injustice!") The devout Christian who composed *Beowulf* could never have uttered directly such a desperate sentiment as this, but through the indirections of poetry he has suggested something very like it. For the tone and emphasis of his poem seem to tell us no less forcefully than Unamuno could have done that if it is oblivion that is reserved for such heroes as Beowulf, then these men lived their lives in such a way that this will have been an injustice.

Fred C. Robinson
Yale University

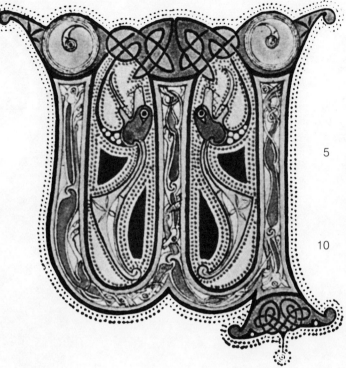

HAT
of the Spear-Danes in days of yore?
We have heard of the glory of the great folk-leaders,
how those athelings* did arduous deeds!

Often Shield Shefing shattered the courage
5   of troops of marauders by taking their mead-seats.
He terrified those nobles—long after the time
he appeared as a foundling. Comfort for that fate
came when he grew and prospered in glory
until those who lived in the neighboring lands
10 over the whale's road had to obey him,
yield him tribute. Yes—a good king!

Later a boy was born to Shield,
a young lad in his house, the hope of the Danes,
whom God had sent them, perceiving their need,
15 how they had suffered with no king to sustain them
for far too long. The Lord of Life,
the Wielder of Glory, gave worldly honor
to Shield's son among the South-Danes.
Beowulf** was famous—his glory spread far.
20 Thus a young warrior should strive to be worthy:
giving freely, while still in his father's care.
In later days, then, friends will leap
to stand beside him when strife comes—
companions will serve him. By praiseworthy deeds
25 a man shall prosper among people everywhere.

* *athelings:* noblemen

* *Not the hero of the poem, who is introduced at line 194.

2   Shield, when old and his hour had come,
turned away into the Lord's protection.
His loving companions carried him out
to the ocean's edge as he had ordered

30   when still he could speak as the Shielding's lord;
long had that dear prince ruled in the land.
Shining in the harbor, a ring-prowed ship
stood icy and eager, the atheling's vessel.
There they laid their beloved lord,

35   their giver of rings, that glorious man,
on the deck by the mast among many treasures,
fine things from foreign lands.

Never was ship more nobly adorned
with battle weapons and garments of war,

40   with blades and with byrnies! * On his breast they laid
many a gift that would go with him
in his far wanderings over the waves.
They girded him round with ancient gold
more generously on that final journey

45   than those folk did who set him adrift
alone on chill seas when only a child.
At the last they set up a golden standard
high over his head, then let the waves have him—
gave him to the sea. Their hearts were sad

50   and mournful their minds, for men cannot know,
neither hall-councillors nor heroes under Heaven,
how to say what hands received that cargo.

byrnies: mail coats

Then in the strongholds the son of Shield,
Beowulf the Dane, grew dear to his people

55 as a famous king when his father, in dying,
had gone from the land. Late in life
he sired Halfdane, who held the proud Shieldings
until gray with age, a grim old warrior.
Four sons and daughters he fathered all told,

60 and brought them up to be great rulers:
Heorogar and Hrothgar and Halga the Good,
and an excellent daughter, who was Onla's queen,
beloved wife of the Swedish war-king.

Then Hrothgar was granted glory in battle,

65 success in the field, which ensured that his friends
obeyed him eagerly, until that band grew
to a mighty troop. It came to his mind then
that he would command that a huge mead building
be made for his warriors, a mighty hall

70 which the sons of men should hear of forever.
And he would apportion out to his people
all that God had given him,
except for shared lands and the lives of men.

4

75 I have heard that then through the whole world
craftsmen of many kinds were ordered
to make that place fair. In due course it befell
that Hrothgar's pride and joy was completed,
the greatest of halls. He named it Heorot—
his word was law throughout the land.

80 He kept his vow and gave rings of value
as banquet treasures. The building towered
high and wide-gabled—awaiting the hostile
leap of flames. But it was a long time yet
before the sword-hatred of a son-in-law

85 should wake to avenge a wicked slaughter.

In these days a spirit who dwelt in darkness
was growing more agonized in his anger
each time that he heard the joy in the hall
ring out anew. The round-harp hummed,

90 the clear song of the *shope*. * He sang who knew well
about the ancient beginnings of men.
He said the Almighty made the world,
the shining plain encircled by water,
exulting set out the sun and moon

95 as lamps to give light to land dwellers,
and fairly adorned the fields of earth
with limbs and leaves. Then he made life
for every kind of creature that moves.
And so the lordly ones lived in delight

100 and happy ease, until One began
to perform evil deeds, a fiend from Hell—
that grim spirit was called Grendel!

shope: minstrel

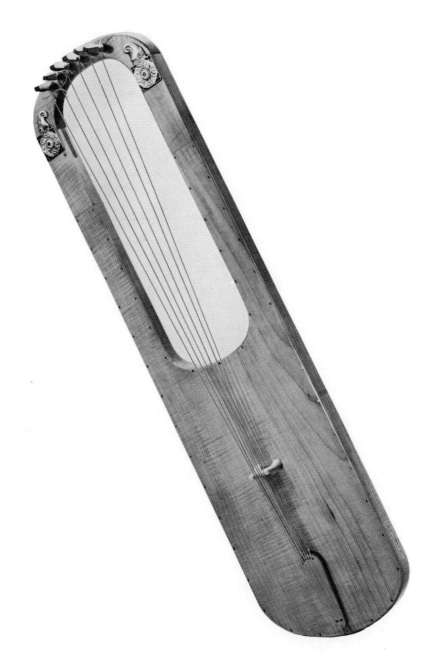

105 *Long he lived mournful in demon's lair*
after the Creator had cast out Cain
and all his kindred for the killing of Abel—
the Lord everlasting avenged that blow!
No joy had Cain in that jealous feud
110 *when the Maker had driven him far from mankind.*
From his loins were born the uncanny beings,
giants and orcs and evil elves,
and also the titans who long contended
against God. He gave them their due!

2. The Coming of Grendel

115 The fall of night brought Grendel forth
to see how the Danes, with their drinking done,
had gone to rest in that gabled hall.
He found there, sleeping after the feast,
a band of warriors, quite unaware
120 of the woes of men—so the vengeful monster,
grim in his wrath, was ready at once
to rage upon them! From rest he plucked
thirty thanes, and, thrilled with his plunder,
darted away to his own den,
125 making for home with a sackful of murder.

When dawn came, the light of day
revealed Grendel's skill at slaughter;
and then festivity turned to woe—
sad songs in the morning. Mighty Hrothgar,
130 that famous ruler, wrapped in anguish,
wept at the death of his warrior-thanes.
Others found the monster's footprints,
a signature that foretold a strife
too long, too difficult. And without delay,

6 135 the next night, indeed, he began anew
           with more killing, and had no qualms
           about that feud—he was too fixed on it!
           Then he who sought a sleeping place
           somewhere else was easy to find—
    140 in the women's bowers. For who would brave
           the violence of that new hall-vassal
           once he had seen it?

                                        They kept themselves then
           at a safer distance away from the demon,
           and Grendel ruled and raged against mankind,
    145 alone and evil, until empty stood
           the best of houses. That was a hard time,
           twelve long winters of bitter woe.
           The king of the Danes had to endure
           this cruel affliction, and it became
    150 as familiar to the sons of men
           as a well-known song, that Grendel waged
           war against Hrothgar, with hateful attacks
           and murderous forays for many a season,
           a permanent feud. He wanted no peace.
    155 To stop killing the Danish kindred
           or settle with gold was no goal of his—
           no hall-lord had any reason to hope
           for bright compensation from that slayer's hand!
           No, that demon, that dark death-shadow,
    160 leapt out upon young and old alike,
           a hideous ambush! In darkness he held
           the misty moors. Men cannot know
           whither such hell-wights bend their ways!

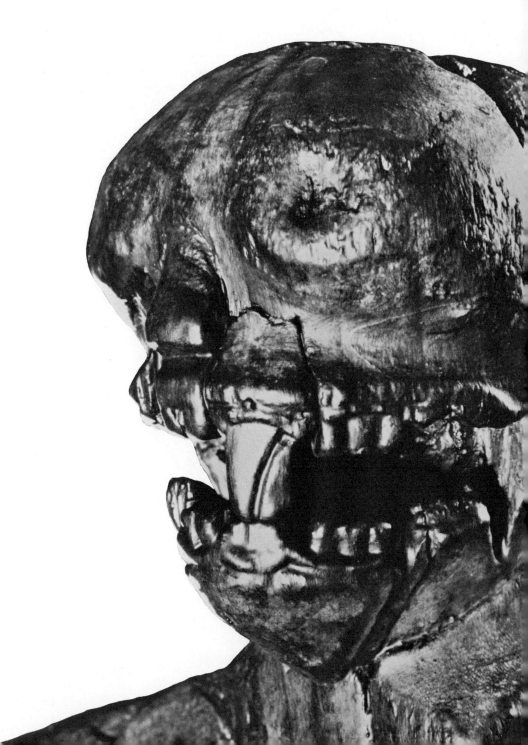

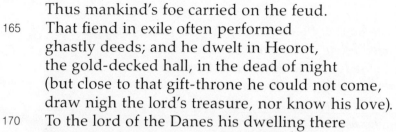

Thus mankind's foe carried on the feud.
165　That fiend in exile often performed
　　ghastly deeds; and he dwelt in Heorot,
　　the gold-decked hall, in the dead of night
　　(but close to that gift-throne he could not come,
　　draw nigh the lord's treasure, nor know his love).
170　To the lord of the Danes his dwelling there
　　was heart-breaking torment. Others took
　　more active council: they cast about
　　in secret to discover what could be done
　　to stem the tide of sudden attacks.
175　At times they vowed in idol-tents
　　to sacrifice, in ancient phrases
　　seeking aid from the slayer of souls
　　in their deep sorrow.

8

Such was their wont,
the hope of the heathens; in their hearts they thought of
180 *Hell below. They knew not the Lord,*
the Judge of Deeds, or how to rejoice
in trusting God, the Protector in Heaven,
the Wielder of Glory. Woe be to him
who because of strife must shove his soul
185 *to the heart of the fire! He cannot hope*
for help or change, ever. Happy is he
who may seek out the Lord on his last day
and ask for peace in the Father's embrace!

3. Beowulf Goes to the Land of the Danes

Despite his wisdom, Halfdane's son
190 could not stop turning over his troubles
in that painful time, or suppress his worry—
the strife was too cruel that had stricken his people,
a grim persecution, the greatest night-terror.
But Grendel's deeds were told to a Geat
195 in his far homeland, to Hygelac's thane. *

He was the mightiest man in the world
in those long ago days of this fleeting life,
and noble of purpose. He ordered prepared
a goodly ship, and said he would go
200 over the swan's road to seek out Hrothgar,
knowing that prince had need of men.
His wise friends did not find fault
with him for that daring, though he was dear to them;
indeed, they encouraged him, casting lots
205 for his coming venture, and the valiant fighter
chose from among the Geatish champions
the bravest he could find. Then Beowulf went forth
as one of fifteen, a sea-crafty warrior
who showed them, by landmarks, the way to his ship.

* *thane:* sworn follower

210 The moments passed; the men waited.
When the vessel was well afloat on the waves
they clambered aboard beside the cliff
where the currents whirled, carrying treasures
into that hold, handsome weapons
215 and splendid armor. Then they cast off
on a willing journey in their ship of wood.

Thrust by the wind over billowing waves,
it flew through the foam as free as a bird,
and sailed so far by the following day
220 that sailors perched in that twisted prow
could make out the shining shapes of land:
bright seacliffs, broad headlands,
then sharp rocky crags. They had crossed the ocean;
the voyage was over. Eagerly now,
225 they leapt ashore to anchor their ship,
their ring-mail singing as they moved around.
But they paused to give their thanks to God
for an easy passage on the perilous sea.

From the high sea wall someone was watching;
230 the Shielding whose task was to guard that shore
saw them lift their shields from the side of the ship,
ready for battle. Bursting with curiosity,
wondering what kind of men these were,
Hrothgar's sentinel leapt to his saddle,
235 rode down to the shore, and shook his spear
in a mighty fist, though his words were formal:
"Who are you, coming here in armor,
a band of men in byrnies, steering
your high-keeled ship down the ocean streets,
240 across the water? Look, I have watched here

at this land's end for a long time
to make certain that no sea-invader
would disembark on the Danish shore,
and never have warriors borne weapons here
245 more openly! Nor do you offer
any sign of the elders' consent.
And never in the world have I seen a more noble
man in armor tower above others
than him in your midst; that is no mere hall-thane
250 made proud with weapons—may his appearance
never prove false! But now, inform me
of your kindred before you come any farther
on Danish soil—you might be spies!
Listen to me, sea-faring men
255 far from your homes, I have one thought,
and here it is: you had better hurry
and tell me clearly where you have come from!''

4. His Reply to the Sentinel's Challenge

The leader among them made his reply,
wisely unlocked his hoard of words:
260 "You are looking at men from the land of the Geats;
we are Hygelac's hearth companions.
My father, familiar to men everywhere,
was a noble prince whose name was Edgetheow.
He lived many winters before passing away,
265 aged and honored; the elders who offer
advice to kings recall him well.
With friendly intent we have come very far
to seek your lord, the son of Halfdane,
guide of his people. Give us advice!
270 How shall we approach your proud leader
to make known our mission? There can be nothing

secret about it, for surely you know
whether it is true, as we have been told,
that among the Danes some dire being
275   shows hatred by his deeds in the dead of night;
uncannily hostile, he causes terror
with a grim corpse-hunger! I have come to Hrothgar
to offer help with an open heart,
to aid that good king in overcoming
280   the fiend—if change from this evil affliction
can ever grant him relief again—
and then his burning cares will be cooler;
or else he will have to endure forever
a life of distress, so long as there stands
285   the best of houses in its high place!"

The sentinel spoke where he sat before them,
brave on his warhorse: "Words and deeds
are two things that an intelligent man
must learn to assess if he means to succeed.
290   I hear you tell me that you intend
loyal service to the Shielding's lord.
Come then, with your weapons; I will show you the way.
Moreover, my thanes will be ordered to guard
your freshly tarred ship, to shield it well
295   against all marauders while it rests by the shore—
until the time comes that its coiled prow
is launched on the currents to carry you back
across the waves to Weathermark,
along with those brave men you have brought
300   who have the luck to survive with their lives!"
Then he turned his horse. Behind them remained
the roomy vessel bound by a rope,
lying at anchor.

Likenesses of boars
above their cheekplates, bright with gold,
305   shone wondrously, warlike shapes
keeping guard over life. The Geats hurried,
marching together until they could glimpse
that great timbered hall with its golden roof.
No building there was in all the world
310   more famous than this ruler's fortress—
its light shone out over many lands!

Pointing the way to that warriors' hall,
the sentinel instructed them
how to approach it, then turning his horse,
315   bade them farewell in a few words:
"Now I must go. May God almighty
hold you with honor and keep you unharmed
in your brave venture. Back to the sea
I must go to keep watch against invaders."

5. The Road to Heorot

320   Down the wide path paved with stone
the men walked together. Their byrnies gleamed;
the hand-locked rings in that hardy armor
sang as the warriors went along
the road to the the hall. When they arrived there,
325   tired from seafaring, they set down their shields,
wondrously strong, against the wall,
then sank to the bench. Again their byrnies
rang out in song, and the spears stood
all together where the Geats had placed them,
330   an ash-grove with iron-gray leaves. Those athelings
had worthy weapons!

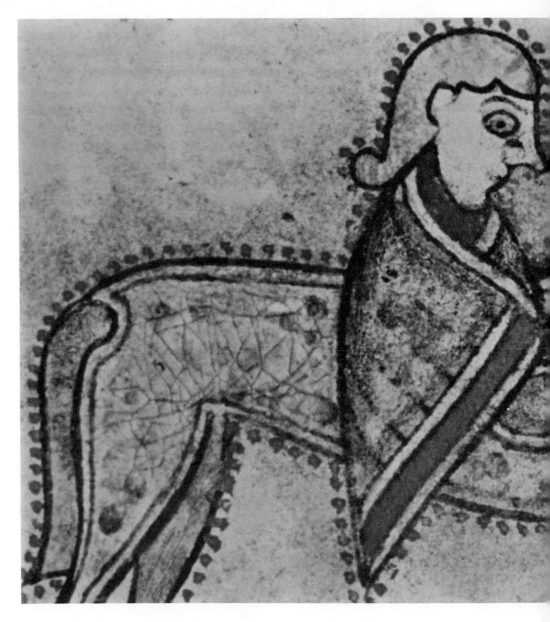

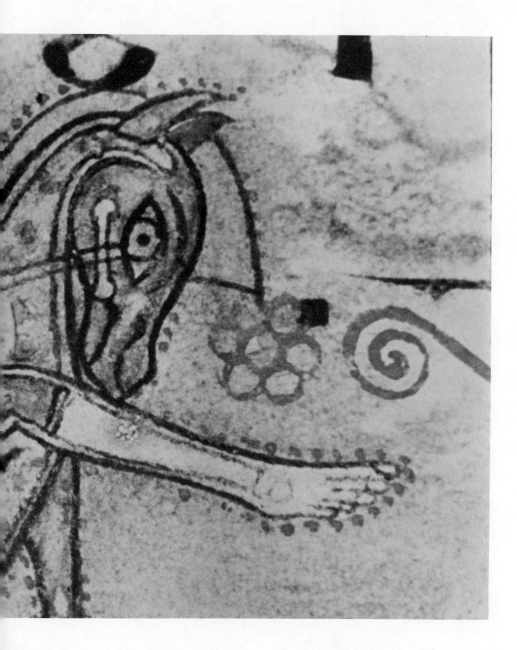

Then a warrior came out
to inquire of the strangers what their kindred was.
"Whence do you bring those brilliant shields,
gray sarks * and grim masked helmets,

335   and all those iron spears? I am Hrothgar's
official spokesman, and may I say
that I've never seen a troop more bravely attired?
I suspect neither exile nor piracy
will have prompted your coming, but courage and pride

340   have led you to Hrothgar."

                 Their leader answered,
selecting his words in a lordly manner,
strong under his helmet: "We are Hygelac's
boon companions. Beowulf is my name.
I wish to tell Halfdane's son himself,

345   that noble ruler, the nature of
the cause that brings me, if he will accord us
the honor of approaching such a princely man."

Wulfgar spoke; a high-ranking Wendel,
his clever mind was known to many,

350   along with his prowess in war, and his wisdom:
"I shall inquire of our king,
the friend and lord of the Danish folk
and their giver of rings, about granting you
leave to approach him, our famous leader,

355   and I shall return at once to tell you
whatever it pleases him to reply."

* sarks: mail coats

14   Quickly he strode to where the king
     sat inside, with his silver hair
     shining among friends; before his shoulder
360 Wulfgar, according to noble custom,
     stood, and spoke freely to his friendly lord:
     "We have visitors who have voyaged far
     to come here, sir, seafaring Geats.
     The leader of these athelings
365 is called Beowulf, and they request
     permission to enter, that they might hold speech
     with my noble lord. Do not deny them
     a kindly answer, O gracious king!
     In war equipment they appear worthy
370 of our esteem. Indeed, that earl
     did well who guided these warriors hither."

Hrothgar spoke, lord of the Shieldings:
"Beowulf? I knew him when he was a boy.
His father was Edgetheow. For his fealty
King Hrethel gave him the Geatish princess,
375 his own daughter, to adorn his home.
Now his son comes seeking our friendship.
Already those who rove the seas
bearing our courtesy gifts to the Geats,
bright treasures of gold, tell tales of him,
380 that he has the might of thirty men
in the grip of his hand. Perhaps holy God
has sent him to us as a sign of hope
for the West Danes—would this were true!—
against Grendel's horror. To that good man
385 I shall offer gifts to honor his courage.
Go now, quickly, tell them to come in
and see how good kinsmen gather together.
Say also these words: their coming is welcome
to the Danish people!"

                              Turning to the door,
390 Wulfgar spoke from just inside:
"My master, the lord of the Danes, commands me
to say he knows your noble lineage,
and invites you, who have so bravely ventured
across the waves, to be welcome here.
395 You may enter, in all your war-equipment,
even your helmets, to approach Hrothgar;
but let your shields and those dangerous shafts
await out here the result of your words."

16

400 Beowulf arose then, and around him his men,
a notable troop; he entrusted some
with guarding the weapons while he went inside.
They marched together as the messenger led them
under Heorot's roof. The hardy warrior
went in his helmet to stand on the hearth,
405 where his byrnie sparkled as he spoke
(that battle-net linked with a smith's lively skill):
"Health to Hrothgar! I am Hygelac's
kinsman and thane. Many things I have done
that are famous already. This affair of Grendel
410 was related to me in my own land
by travelers, who told us that this timbered hall,
the best of buildings, made for brave men,
stands empty and useless when the evening light,
fair in the heavens, fades from the sky.

415 "My own kinsmen and the wisest of the councillors,
and the best among us, O mighty Hrothgar,
persuaded me that I should seek you
because they knew my enormous strength,
and had seen my courage that time when I came
420 bloody from a fight where I captured five
of our huge enemies in a hard battle,
then killed, by night, a number of sea monsters,
totally crushed them—they had courted trouble!—
avenging the Geats. Now it is Grendel's turn.
425 Now I should like to hold, alone,
a meeting with that monster, if you will permit me.
Chief of the Danes, champion of the Shieldings,
I ask one boon (do not forbid me!):
Allow me, noble lord of warriors,
430 protector of the folk, now I have come so far,
to attempt alone, with only my troop,
this brave company, to cleanse Heorot!

"And because I gather that Grendel rashly
spurns all weapons, I also wish
435 (in order to please my own dear prince
Hygelac, and make him proud of me)
to lay aside my shining sword
and yellow shield, and show that demon
a fight to the death, foe against foe,
440 with my grip alone! Then he who loses
must give himself up to the judgment of God.

"But if that fiend should win the fight
in this place of battle, I think that upon
the Geats he will feed . . . as on Danish folk
445 he has often been sated. So you need not consider
where to hide my head, for he will have me
dripping with blood, if death takes me.
He will bear me away, his mouth watering,
to taste my flesh, tearing it ruthlessly,
450 staining the moors. So do not distress
yourself concerning my body, but send
this best of byrnies, if battle takes me,
to Hygelac, for it is Hrethel's heirloom,
the work of Wayland, that I wear on my breast,
455 the finest of garments. Fate goes as it must!"

Hrothgar spoke, lord of the Shieldings:
"Both from duty, my friend Beowulf,
and a sense of kindness you have come to us.
Your father started the greatest of feuds
460   when by his own hand he slew Heatholaf
among the Wylfings; the Geats were wary
of defending their friend with a feud in the offing,
so he came away to the kingdom of the Danes,
overseas to the Shieldings, and they sheltered him.
465   All this happened when, as a youth,
I had just come to power in the jewelled kingdom,
the bright stronghold of the Danes. My brother
Heorogar had died, a son of Halfdane
born before me; he was better than I!
470   But I settled that feud by sending gifts
to the Wylfings over the water's ridge.
I sent them treasures, and he swore me oaths.

"Hard it is to say from my heart
to any man what misery,
475   what havoc Grendel has wrought with his hatred,
what harm he has done us. My dear hall-troop
of warriors has waned; *wyrd* * has swept them
into Grendel's power. But God may easily
deprive that desperate foe of deeds!

* *wyrd:* fate

480 Often it has been that able men
have boasted loudly over their beer
that they would defy the fiend's attack
with fierce blades, and hold the hall—
and then in the morning there would only remain
485 the marks of their blood on this noble building,
the planks of the benches painted with gore,
the hall, with their lives. Of loyal men
I would have the fewer when that fight was done . . .

"Sit now to the feast and unfetter your thoughts,
490 pledge great deeds as your mood may prompt you!"
Then room was made in that friendly mead-hall
for all the Geats to sit together
on the drinking benches, and those doughty men
went to their places. A thane was watchful
495 of their every need, and from the ale-vessel
poured shining liquid. At times the shope
sang in the hall, and happiness reigned
over all that gathering of Danes and Geats.

8. Unferth's Taunt

Unferth spoke; the son of Edgelaf,
500 who sat at the feet of the Shielding lord,
unbound his battle-runes.* Beowulf's voyage
and his noble venture rankled enormously,
for Unferth begrudged any greatness in others,
and found it offensive if they earned more fame
505 under the heavens than he himself—:
"Are you that Beowulf who strove against Breca
across the sea in a swimming contest,
where the two of you recklessly risked your lives
on the high seas for a heedless boast?
510 They say that nobody could dissuade you,
neither friend nor foe, from that fruitless act
of wilful pride. You swam through the water,
arching your arms through the ocean currents,
weaving the waves, drawing hand after hand,
515 gliding on the sea; then suddenly the billows
swelled in a storm, and you struggled there
for seven nights. But Breca outswam you;
he had more strength. And a morning dawned
when the tide had hurled him on the Heatho-Raemes' shore.
520 He went on home then, a hero to his people
in the land of the Brondings where he belonged,
and was soon entrusted with treasure and kingdom
in that mighty fortress. In his match against you,
Breca entirely fulfilled his boast.
525 I wonder if you will not come off the worse
in this venture, too (though you have prevailed
in many grim battles), if you dare to remain
waiting in this hall for a whole night."

*This colorful phrase means merely that Unferth "began to speak brusquely."

Beowulf spoke, the son of Edgetheow:

530 "Well, Unferth, my friend, being full of beer,
you have much to say about my swim
with Breca! But truly I tell you this:
my strength was greater against the sea
and the angry waves than any other man's.

535 The two of us vowed, being very young—
we were both only boys when we made this boast—
to venture out on the wild ocean
and dare to risk our lives. And we did it!
As we breasted the waves, we held naked blades

540 fiercely in our hands to defend ourselves
against the great whales. Breca could not gain
any distance from me in that mighty current
through the speed of his stroke, nor did I wish to spurt
away from him, so together in the waves

545 we swam for five nights, until swept asunder
by the swelling waters of the coldest weather,
as night grew dark and a wind from the north
turned wildly against us.

                                    "The rough waves
aroused the fury of the great fishes,

550 and there my hand-locked mail helped me;
my byrnie defended me from those foes,
where, woven for battle, it lay on my breast
adorned with gold. Drawing me down,
a fierce monster held me fast

555 in his ugly grip. But it was granted
that I should touch that beast with the tip
of my blade, and the storm of battle destroyed
the huge sea-creature through my hand . . .

"Those predators, pressing in upon me,
560   harassed me sorely. But I served them well
and justly with my jewelled sword.
At their feast below those foul spoilers
had little pleasure; they had planned to partake
of me, at their banquet on the ocean bottom!
565   But the following morning they were flotsam, lying
along the shore, put to sleep by my blade,
hurt so severely that voyagers
have never since been hindered in sailing
their ships on those seas. From the east shone
570   God's bright beacon; the billowing waves
grew calm, and then I saw cliffs ahead,
a windy land. *Wyrd* often saves
the undoomed hero if his courage holds!

"In the end my sword appeared to have slain
575   nine sea-beasts. Never have I heard of
a harder night battle under heaven's vault,
nor a man more forlorn among the waves;
but I survived the violent clutch
of those foes, and weary from the fight was swept
580   by the flooding tides onto Finnmark shores,
left high and dry.

"I have not heard
that you have brandished your flashing blade
in battles so wild. Breca has never,
nor indeed, either of you, yet done
585   anything comparable in the way of conflict
with the blood-gleaming sword—I do not boast overmuch—
though one must remember your brother's murder,
and he your own kinsman! For that deed, Hell
will claim you someday, clever though you are.

590   "I say to you truly, son of Edgelaf,
that demon would never have done so many
crimes so insulting to your king,
such harm in Heorot, if your own heart
were half so brave as you yourself boast;
595   he has found out that he need not fear
an avenging storm of violent blades,
the feuding swords of the brave Shieldings.
He takes his toll, sparing none
of the Danish people, takes his pleasure,
600   puts them to death and expects no reprisal
from the Danes of the Spear. But soon enough
I shall show him the strength and courage
of a Geatish warrior! And whoever wishes
can go bravely to mead after tomorrow's
605   morning light shines for men,
when the radiant sun rises in the south!"
Then Hrothgar, the giver of rings, was glad.
The brave old chieftain of the Bright Danes,
the leader of those people, who had longed for help,
610   had faith in Beowulf's firm resolution.

When the jesting of heroes rose joyously
and words were winsome, Wealtheow came forth,
Hrothgar's queen, mindful of kinship.
That gold-laden lady, greeting the men,
615   handed the cup around the hall,
first to the lord who guarded that land,
the dear home of his people. She bade him take pleasure
in his drink from the cup, and the noble king
gladly partook of the shining goblet.
620   Then the Helming lady went through the hall
to young and old, letting each man use
the cup in his turn, until the time came
that the ring-laden queen in courtesy
bore the mead-cup to Beowulf.
625   She greeted the prince, and piously thanked God
that the course she desired had come to pass—
that now she could count on someone for comfort
from the wicked deeds.

                    The fierce warrior
accepted the cup that the queen held out.
630   He drank, and then, sonorous, inspired by the challenge,
Beowulf spoke, Edgetheow's son:
"I resolved, when first I set out to sea,
when I boarded that ship with my band of men,
that I would fully perform the wish
635   of your people, or fall in the fight, caught fast
in that horrible claw. I shall behave
with fitting courage, or my final day
shall come to meet me in this mead-hall!"
The woman liked well those noble words
640   of the Geat's pledge; gold-laden she went
to sit in splendor beside her lord.

Then, as before, the sounds were fair
inside that hall, the warriors happy,
their tales brave, until the time came
645 that Halfdane's son wanted to seek
his evening rest; he knew that the enemy
had longed to do battle in that high building
from the time they had seen the sun's first light
until nightfall lengthened across the land
650 and shadows came moving in dark shapes
under the clouds.

                   The company all rose.
Hrothgar the king spoke to his hero,
offering Beowulf the best of luck,
and rule of his wine-hall, saying these words:
655 "I have never entrusted to another man,
so long as I have been able to lift my shield,
lordship in this hall but to you alone.
Take now and hold the best of houses,
remember fame, hold fast to valor,
660 watch against the foe! You shall want for nothing,
if you come through alive from this deed of courage!"

10. The Watch for Grendel

Then out from Heorot Hrothgar went,
the lord of the Shieldings, with his loyal thanes;
the old warrior wanted to seek his wife,
665 his consort Wealtheow, and the comfort of bed.

Men soon discovered that the King of Glory,
in special dispensation, had set a hall-watch
against Grendel, a guard against giants.
In his great strength the prince of the Geats
670 trusted fully—and in God's friendship.
That warrior removed his woven mail-coat,
the helmet from his head, and handed his sword,
the finest iron blade, to a friendly thane,
bade him take care of that battle gear.

675 Then Beowulf, before he climbed into his bed,
reflected on some of his former words:
"I take no less pride in my martial prowess,
in my hardy fighting, than Grendel in his.
Thus with the sword I shall not slay him,
680 kill him with that weapon, though I certainly could;
he would not understand how to strike back
with blade against shield, though he is brave enough
in his wicked strength. So this night we abstain
from the sword altogether, if Grendel dares seek
685 a war without weapons, and then wise God,
the holy Lord, on whichever hand
seems fitting, will assign the victor's fame."

Putting his face to the pillow, the warrior
began to rest, and around him many
690 a brave man sank to sleep in the hall.
Not one of those thanes thought for a moment
that he would live to return to his beloved
home, his kindred, and the hall he was raised in;

they had been told that death had taken
695   very many before them in that mead-hall,
too many good Danes. But the Maker granted
that the fight of the Weathergeats would be woven
with battle victory, that they would vanquish
their strange foe through the strength of one,
700   through his own power. Truly, forever,
mighty God has ruled mankind;
this is known.

                     In the night he came—
the shadow walker! The warriors slept
who were trusted to guard that gabled hall,
705   all but one. This was known also:
that Grendel could not, when God did not wish it,
draw them under the demon shadow.
But one man lay there, watchful, and waiting
in anger for the enemy and the outcome of that fight.

11. The Fight with Grendel

710   From the moor there came, under misty cliffs,
Grendel striding; he bore God's wrath.
The monster of evil had it in mind
to hunt for his dinner in that high hall!
Under the masses of cloud he moved
715   until he could glimpse the gleams of gold
that marked those timbers. That was not the first time
that he had visited Hrothgar's home,
but never before had he found in that place
a fiercer welcome, or warriors more fiery!

720 To the hall he came, huge and striding,
doomed, without joy. At once the door
sprang from its hinges at the touch of that hand.
He burst open the building's mouth,
cruel in his rage, and quickly then
725 he stepped across the colored floor,
moving in fury, as from his eyes
there leapt a horrible light like a flame.

Within that mead-hall he saw many men,
kinsmen, sleeping calmly together,
730 loyal companions. Then his heart leapt up:
that terrible demon intended to tear
each comrade's life, before daylight came,
away from his body. The thought of a banquet
made his mouth water. But *wyrd* would not
735 let him enjoy that taste any longer
after that night.

                    The noble kinsman
of Hygelac watched to see how the wicked
predator meant to plan his attack.
That loathsome demon would not delay;
740 like a flash, he snatched up the first of his quarry,
a sleeping man, and slit him open,
bit his body, gulped down his blood,
swallowed huge morsels, immediately
had devoured each part of his victim's corpse
745 to his fingers and toes!

nearer now, clutched at the next with his claw,
stirred from his rest a stronger man!
As the demon reached out, the other grasped him,
and grimly sat up against that arm.
750 And then that cruel fiend first discovered
that he had never met, throughout middle earth,
in any warrior in all the world,
a mightier grip. In his heart he grew
greatly afraid—but he could not flee.
755 His single thought was to slip into darkness,
back among his devils; those earlier days
of gluttony here were gone forever.

High of courage, Hygelac's kinsman
remembered his evening's speech, stood up,
760 gripped fast against him; fingers burst;
Grendel was desperate to get away,
but the prince came closer. The monster in panic
felt like swinging free if he could,
then breaking for the fen, but he knew that his fingers
765 were caught in that grip. That was a dismal call
for the harmful fiend, that he paid to Heorot!

The hall thundered, sounding to the thanes
who lived in that place hideously like
the pleasure of men who were merry on ale.
770 Both were furious. The floor boomed.
Then it was a wonder that the noble wine-hall
held out so well against those warriors,
that it did not fall. But it was made fast
within and without with iron bands
775 designed by a clever smith. From the sill

at the floor of the building where those fierce ones fought
benches lavish with gold sprang loose.
No wise man among the Shieldings
had ever expected that anyone
780   could break that beautiful antlered building
or pull it apart, unless pulsing flames
were to swallow it up.

                       The sound roared out,
gaining in frenzy, pouring out fear
for all of the Danes, for each of those
785   who heard that wailing come through the wall,
the mournful tune of God's antagonist,
his song, not of victory—the slave of Hell
bemoaning his fate. He held him fast
who was the mightiest man in the world
790   in those long ago days of this fleeting life.

12. The Quelling of Grendel

For nothing in the world did Beowulf want
to let that killer escape alive,
nor did he consider that Grendel had served
any useful purpose! A daring youth
795   from the band of warriors came slashing about
with his ancient sword; he wanted to save
the life, if he could, of his noble leader.
And others joined him, just as brave,
but unaware when they drew their weapons—
800   intending to hew Grendel down between them,
to get at his life—that none of the greatest
iron blades over all the earth,
not any sword at all, could ever touch him;

he had cast a spell on all cutting edges,
805   making them harmless. Yet his departure,
in those long ago days, from this fleeting life,
would be grippingly painful, and that grim spirit
would be forced to descend to the fires of the damned.

Then he who had perpetrated such horrors,
810   so many crimes against mankind,
the fiend who was waging a permanent feud
with God, found that his garment of flesh
would no longer serve him, for the noble kinsman
of Hygelac had gripped him hard by the hand
815   (each was loathsome to the other alive),
and was pulling his body to pieces, cracking
his shoulder wide open. Sinews sprang out
and the body burst apart! Beowulf was victor,
and the demon Grendel in his death-throes
820   sought only to flee far into the wilds
to his joyless den, for there was no doubt,
he knew, that his life, the number of his days,
was done. For all the Danes, that conflict
had been settled according to their desire:
825   he who had come from so far had cleansed
Hrothgar's hall, and from hateful intrusions
had rescued it.

            He revelled in his deed,
in the work of that night, for nobly had he
fulfilled his pledge. The prince of the Geats
830   had entirely undone the distress of the Danes
that had bound them up in endless brooding
and caused them, of sad necessity,
to endure such sorrow. The clear sign of this
came when that hand was placed by the hero
835   with arm and shoulder, all in one piece,
Grendel's whole grip, up under the gable.

Then in the morning many a warrior
hastened to that gift hall, as I have heard;
noble men came from far and near,

840   from all over the land, to look on that marvel,
the foe's huge footprints. His fall seemed
no cause for regret to any of the councillors
who looked on the tracks of the loser of that fight
and saw how weary of mind he was

845   as he made his way thence. To the monsters' tarn,
fated and fleeing, he bent his way.
The water there was welling with blood,
a terrible surf that was swirling up
in burning waves of hot battle gore.

850   Joyless, forlorn and despairing of life,
he hid his doomed and heathen soul
in the harboring fen. There Hell took him.

Afterwards the troop of old companions
and the younger men, too, turned to pleasure,

855   warriors riding away from the pool,
glorious on their horses. The heroic deed
of Beowulf was spoken of, and many men said
that north or south between the two seas,
across the whole earth, there existed no other

860   warrior so brave, more worthy of rule,
under the vast vault of the heavens!
Yet their own prince, Hrothgar, they did not disparage
by such regard, for he was a good king.

At times those riders gave free rein
865 to their roan stallions, let them race,
let them leap forth where the turf seemed fair,
in a test of speed. At times the king's thane,
a splendid man who remembered old songs
and kept them in his mind along with many
870 long ago sayings, began linking his words,
binding them together. Soon he began
to recite with discernment Beowulf's success,
and skillfully to adapt an appropriate story,
mingling his words.

                         He said all there was
875 that he had heard of about the heroic
deeds of Sigemund, the strange things that happened
on the wide travels of that son of Waels—
feuds and crimes that few men
would have heard about, if there had not been
880 Fítela with him in later frays,
when Sigemund would say to his sister's son
something of such feats as they fought together,
always companions in the play of swords;
they killed many giants.

                         To Sigemund came
885 the glory due him after his death,
for that hero had slain a mighty serpent,
the guardian of a hoard. Under the gray stone
the atheling's son descended alone
on that fearsome deed, Fítela not with him.
890 It was granted, however, that his gleaming sword
should strike through that dragon to stand in the wall
quivering, and the beast was destroyed by that blow!

So fearlessly had the warrior performed
that now he could enjoy the hoard of jewels
895   at his own leisure. He loaded his boat.
Wael's son carried that glimmering wealth
into the hold; and the hot beast shrivelled.

In deeds of prowess (for which he prospered),
Sigemund was the most famous of warriors,
900   *of protectors or fighters, among all folk*
since King Heremod's glory declined
with his might and his courage. Among the Jutes
Heremod was betrayed by his own retainers
to men who killed him. Keen were the sorrows
905   *that had long oppressed him, and to his people*
he had grown to be the greatest of burdens.
Many a warrior mourned his exploits,
lamenting for those days when he had believed
that Heremod could not fail as a cure for affliction,
910   *that he would thrive as a prince among thanes*
in his father's pattern, ruling the people
and the kingdom's wealth, its fortress and warriors,
the country of the Shieldings. The kinsman of Hygelac,
Beowulf, became a help to his comrades
915   *and to all, but hatred took hold of the other.*

At times, racing down the yellow roads,
they matched their horses. Then the morning light
moved on, and many a man of valor
hastened to that high hall to see
920   the curious trophy; likewise the king,
the keeper of the hoard, came from his wife's house.
He walked along firm in his warrior's glory,
known well to be best, and his queen walked with him
across the meadow with an escort of maidens.

925   Hrothgar spoke—he went to the hall,
stepped onto the raised place and looked at the roof
adorned with gold, and at Grendel's hand—:
"For this great sight may we give our thanks
to God Almighty! I have endured many
930   afflictions from Grendel, but the Keeper of Glory
can always work wonder after wonder.

"It was not long ago that I gave up hope,
gave up expecting ever to experience
relief from misery, when marked with blood
935   the best of houses stood humbled by horrors—
a far-reaching woe to the men of wisdom,
for they had lost trust in their power to protect
the stronghold of the folk from foes like demons
and wicked spirits. But now this warrior
940   through the might of God has managed the deed
that none of us earlier could have ever
contrived with our wits. Indeed, that woman
who bore, according to noble custom,
such a son, if still she lives,
945   well may declare that wise God
blessed that birth!

"Now, good Beowulf,
I should like to claim you as my own kinsman,
a son in my heart. Hold well, henceforth,
to our new relationship. You shall know no lack
950   of precious things where I wield power.
I have often granted a gift from the hoard
to honor less worth in a lowlier warrior,
weaker in battle. Now, Beowulf, you
have performed such feats that your fame will live
955   forever and ever. May ancient God
grant you always the grace that he grants you now!"

Beowulf spoke, the son of Edgetheow:
"With kindly intent we came to perform
that deed of valor, to meet with the demon
960   and test the strength of that fearsome stranger.
Yet I wish you had seen him stretched out in death
before your own eyes, in all his trappings!
I meant to bind him immediately
onto his deathbed with a dreadful grip
965   so that under my hand he would lie there, openly
struggling for his life—unless he escaped,
weakened though he was. But the Lord did not want me
to stop him from leaving with his life intact:
I could not hold onto him hard enough—
970   he was too strong. But he had to forsake
his hand, his arm, and his whole shoulder,
to save himself and seek escape.

"That destitute being did not thereby
purchase relief for a longer life
975   haunted by his sins, for his wound holds him
tight in the clutch of terrible pain,
a woeful bond; there he must wait,
that guilty demon, for the Great Judgment,
what Heaven's King decides to decree."

980 Then Edgelaf's son Unferth was altogether
a quieter man in vaunting his courage
when the athelings saw the other's skill
displayed high up: the enemy's hand
with its fearful fingers. In front of each one
985 stood a strong nail very like steel,
the talon of the heathen warrior's hand,
a horrible spike. Everyone said
that no iron blade of noble valor
could ever have touched him, that no trusty sword
990 could have harmed that bloody hand of battle!

15. The Banquet

Then all hands were called to Heorot
to make that hall beautiful. Many were the men
and women, too, by whom that wine-house
was adorned for its guests. Golden shone
995 the weavings on the walls, scenes of wonder
for every person who looked thereon.

That bright interior had been broken to rubble,
though tightly bound in bands of iron;
hinges had sprung open, and only the roof
1000 was intact when the demon turned away,
marked with his deeds, to make his flight,
desperate for life. Death is not easy
to hide away from, try it who will!
For those with souls, by necessity,
1005 must pass, each one, to the place prepared
for all who inhabit human lands,
where the body falls asleep in its narrow bed
after the banquet.

38

Then came the hour
when Hrothgar, the son of Halfdane, decided
1010   that he wanted to sit at the feast himself.
I have never heard of a noble band
comport themselves better in their ring-giver's presence.
Brilliant in their fame, they sank to the benches,
rejoiced at the banquet. Joining in their pleasure
1015   with many a cup of mead in that hall
were two bold kinsmen toasting together,
Hrothgar and Hrothulf. Heorot within
was filled with friends; few were the Danes
who gave any thought then to thickening plots.

1020   Hrothgar presented a golden standard
to Beowulf the Geat, to honor his greatness,
and with that banner a helmet and byrnie;
and then many saw a magnificent sword
borne in to the hero. Beowulf drank
1025   from the cup in the hall; no cause had he
for shame before friends at that treasure-sharing!
I have not heard of many great kings who have made
four golden gifts in friendlier wise
to another man on the ale bench!
1030   Spanning that helmet a crest stood high,
twisted with wires to protect the head
from blows without, so that no hard blade
could wound the warrior who was wearing it
into a fight against violent foes.

1035 The king of athelings then ordered that eight
stallions bright with golden bridles
be led through the hall. On one of those horses
was a fine saddle, finished with gems;
it had been the king's own battle seat

1040 when Hrothgar had wished to test his hand
at sword-play. Never was that warrior known
to retreat from the front when corpses fell!

By now the lord of the Ingwines had lavished
upon the Geat a goodly share

1045 of horses and jewels, and he wished him joy of them.
Thus the hoard guardian honored that hero
with such a bounty of stallions and wealth
that no one can find a fault in his kindness
who holds to the truth of that treasure-giving.

16. Hildeburh's Sorrow

1050 Once again, to each princely warrior
who had braved the sea paths with Beowulf,
Hrothgar gave marvellous gifts on the mead-bench,
heirloom treasures. Then he ordered yet more:
that the man should be honored with gold whom earlier

1055 Grendel had slaughtered, as he would have slain
more Geats and Danes, had not wise God
and that warrior's courage conquered *wyrd*.
The Lord ruled then the lives of men,
as still he does. Thus understanding

1060 and prudence are best, for much must be borne
of good and ill, by anyone
who dwells in this world in these difficult days.

Singing and music swelled together
in the presence of Hrothgar, Halfdane's war prince;
1065   the harp had been strummed to many a story
when the king's shope began to declaim
a formal hall tale in front of the mead-bench,
about Finn's men when disaster befell them,
and that Danish hero, Hnaef of the Shieldings,
1070   who was destined to fall in Frisian slaughter.
Truly, Hildeburh had cause to protest
the good faith of the Jutes. Guiltless, she found herself
deprived of her loved ones at that play of shields—
one son, one brother; wounded by the spear,
1075   they sank to their deaths. That was a sad woman!

Hardly without cause did Hoc's daughter
bemoan her fate when morning came,
when under the sky she could clearly see
the murdered corpses of those she had cared for
1080   most dearly in the world. War also took
all Finn's thanes, save only a few,
so that he was not able in any way
to press Hengest to a fight in this place
or dislodge those Danes who were still alive
1085   with the prince's friend.

                 So the Frisians offered
a compact of peace; they would clear out completely
a second hall and its ruling high seat,
which the Shielding warriors could share with the Jutes;
and at the ring-giving the Frisian ruler
1090   would honor the Danes every day,
offering treasures to Hengest's troop—
just as many of those jewels and weapons
of plated gold as he would give
to deck out the Frisians in their drinking hall.

1095   *Then they swore on either side*
   to keep the peace. To Hengest, the king
   promised with undisputed zeal
   that he would protect that dwindled troop
   with honor and wisdom, and that no man would
1100   *weaken their pact with words or deeds;*
   and no malicious tongues were allowed
   to mention the fact that the Danes were following
   their chieftain's slayer, having no other choice.
   If anyone dared with audacious speech
1105   *to remind the Danes of that deadly hatred,*
   then the sword's edge would settle it!

   The pyre was made ready and precious gold
   carried from the hoard. The hardiest warrior
   of all the Shieldings was laid there, shining,
1110   *where all could see the blood-stained sarks,*
   the iron-hard boar-helmets, overlaid
   with glittering gold, and many good men
   who had died of their wounds. What warriors had fallen!
   Then Hildeburh said that her own son
1115   *should be laid beside Hnaef, and left to the flames;*
   his corpse should be burnt beside his kinsman,
   at his uncle's shoulder. Then singing, she
   lamented her sorrow. The warrior ascended;
   the hugest of fires wound up to the heavens,
1120   *howling by the mound. Heads were consumed;*
   gashes burst open and the blood sprang out
   through bitter wounds. Soon the blaze,
   greediest of spirits, had swallowed the dead
   of both peoples; their power had vanished.

1125 *The Shieldings went forth to find themselves dwellings;*
lamenting their friends, they looked around Frisia
for house and high fortress, for Hengest was forced
to remain with Finn through a mournful winter.
He cast no lots, yet kept on thinking
1130 *of home, though he could not cross the ocean*
on his serpent-prowed ship, for the sea was swollen
with mighty storms; it strove with the wind.
Then winter locked the waves in icy bonds
until spring weather brought warmth again—
1135 *as still it does. The dazzling seasons*
keep their proper times.

                    When the winter had passed
and the land was fair, a longing to go
took hold of that thane. But he gave more thought
to wreaking vengeance than to riding the seas,
1140 *to bringing about a bitter meeting*
that he had in mind for the men of the Jutes.
The choice of revenge, then, was very easy,
when Hunlafing laid upon his lap
"Light of Battle," that best of blades,
1145 *whose edges were known to the Jutish nobles.*

Then cruel were the swords that struck down the king,
Finn the brave-hearted, in his own house,
for Guthlaf and Oslaf had greatly complained
of being attacked after weary traveling—
1150 *and held Finn to blame. The fiery heart*
cannot be subdued; that hall was dyed
red with friends' lives, and the ruler lay
slain among his troop, and the queen was taken.

The Shielding warriors bore to their ship
1155 the ancient treasures that Finn had protected
in his coffers at home—all they could carry
of the precious ornaments. And over the sea paths
they took his lady to the land of the Danes,
led her to her people.

          The lay was sung,
1160 the minstrel's tale, and mirth started up again;
the revels increased as cup-bearers came
pouring the wine. Then Wealtheow came forth
in her golden necklace where the king and his nephew
sat nobly together, still known for their friendship,
1165 each true to the other. And there sat Unferth
at the feet of those princes; they praised and trusted
his great courage, though to his kinsmen
he had done little service at the play of swords.

The lady spoke: "Take this cup, my lord,
1170 giver of rings, gold-friend to men!
Be joyful, and speak with generous words
of kindness to the Geats, in your kingly way.
Be gracious, and remember them with those gifts
from near and far that fill your coffers.
1175 I have been told that you wish to take
this man for your son. But the bright mead-hall,
Heorot, is cleansed. Hand out while you hold them
the kingdom's rewards, but leave to your kinsmen
folk and rule when you must go forth
1180 to discover your fate.

"O friend of the Shieldings,
I know that my gracious Hrothulf will guard
our children with honor, if you are chosen
before your nephew to make your way forth
from life in this world. I expect he will wish
1185 *to repay our sons with special goodness*
if he recalls all the kindnesses
that we showed to him when he was young."

She went along the bench then, to where her boys were,
Hrethric and Hrothmund, and the sons of heroes,
1190 *all the youths together; there sat the Geat,*
Beowulf himself, between those two brothers.

18. The Ring-Giving

Bearing the mead cup, the queen bid Beowulf
in courteous words to partake of that wine,
and his worth was acknowledged with noble treasures:
1195 two arm rings, a corselet, and a golden collar—
the greatest torque I have ever heard tell of.

No, I have not heard of a finer hoard treasure
under the heavens since Hama made off
*with the Brosinga mene * to that bright city*
1200 *(precious figures in a princely setting);*
he turned from Eormenric to eternal gain.
Hygelac of the Geats, Swerting's grandson,
flaunted that collar on his final campaign,
when he strove to protect beneath his standard
1205 *the booty he had won—but* wyrd *took him.*
Because of his pride he had courted trouble,
a feud with the Frisians. On the flowing waves
powerful Hygelac transported that treasure
of fabulous wealth—to fall under his shield.

mene: necklace

1210   *Then three things passed into Frankish power:*
his life, his war-gear, and that wondrous collar.
Less noble were the fighters who, after the feud,
plundered that corpse on the field of carnage—
of havoc for the Geats.

                             But applause had greeted
1215   *the tale of Hama, and then in the hall*
Wealtheow spoke: "Wear this collar,
dear Beowulf, well; let it bring you luck,
and the corselet, too, from the common treasure.
May you show your power, and to these young Shieldings
1220   grant your favor, and I'll not forget you!
You have fought so well that far and near,
forever and ever, men will honor you
as widely as that home of the winds, the sea,
encircles the land. As long as you live,
1225   be happy, young man; with many gifts
I shall recall your deeds. Be kind
to my sons in everything, blessed atheling!

"Here each warrior is true to the other,
disposed to be generous, loyal to his prince.
1230   They are harmonious and courteous men—
having drunk from my cup, they do as I bid!"

She returned to her seat and the banquet continued.
They feasted and drank, unwary of the doom,
the twisting fate determined of yore,
1235 that would strike among them long before morning!
Hrothgar, their leader, went away to his house
to seek his bed. Within that high building
the athelings kept watch, as often before.

They cleared the benches and laid down bolsters,
1240 fluffed up feather-beds. (But one of those friends
lay down on his couch a doomed man!)
They had hung their shields above their heads,
bright on the wall, and over each bench
ready to hand they set their steep helmets
1245 that towered in battle, and their ring-mail byrnies,
their magnificent spears. Such was their custom:
they always kept fit and ready for a fight
at home or afield, eager to help
whenever their lord might look to them
1250 in need. That was truly a noble people!

19. Grendel's Mother Comes

They fell asleep. One man paid sorely
for his evening's rest, as often had happened
when Grendel came to dwell in that gold-hall,
evilly, until an end came to that:
1255 after crimes against others he was killed himself!

But then it was seen that still there lived
another monster, marking time

after Grendel's death, the demon's mother,
a witch of the sea, resenting her sorrow,
1260 one who was wont to dwell underwater
in the cold streams *after Cain sent*
a sharp blade through his own brother,
his father's offspring; he set forth then, fated,
proscribed for his murder from life among men,
1265 *to dwell in the wastelands. From his loins awoke*
the demons of wyrd; *Grendel was one of them,*
that hateful foe who had found at Heorot
a man awake and waiting for the fight.
The horrible being laid hold of Beowulf,
1270 *but he remembered his mighty strength,*
the ample gift that God had given him,
and counted on support and comfort from the Prince
who rules on high. Thus he wrestled
that monster from Hell. Humiliated, then,
1275 *mankind's foe went joyless to find*
a place to die in. And that demon mother,
with her heart as heavy as a hanged man, wanted
to venture to Heorot to avenge her son's death.

She came then to Heorot; in that hall the Danes
1280 were fast asleep. A change of fortune
befell them as she entered—and yet the force
of Grendel's mother amounted to less
than his by as much as a woman's might
is shadowed by the strength of a sword-bearing man—
1285 when that fine weapon forged with the hammer,
the blade with a pattern emblazoned with blood,
strikes out at the boar above the helmet.

Then damascened blades were drawn in the hall,
the swords hanging over the seats, and many

shields held fast in men's fists were raised;
but helmets were forgotten when horror came upon them,
and byrnies left aside.

That sea witch wanted

to escape with her life when she was discovered,
but she carried off in her cruel grip

1295   a noble warrior when she went to the fen.
He was the dearest of Hrothgar's companions,
his truest supporter between the two seas,
a noble shield-warrior of great renown,
whom she took from his bed. Beowulf was not there,

1300   for after the gift-giving he had been guided
to another building for the rest he had earned.
A cry rose in Heorot. She reached for the claw,
taking down that hand from its bloody height.
Sorrow was renewed in the homes of the Shieldings:

1305   that was no bargain, when on both sides
they paid for their feuding with the lives of friends!

Savage was the hatred of that hoary old warrior
when they told him about his best of thanes,
and he knew his dearest companion was dead!

1310   Beowulf was quickly bidden to come
to Hrothgar's dwelling; it was break of day.
Nobly he moved among his men,
a champion among warriors, to where the king waited,
wondering if God would ever grant him

1315   a change from this time of terrible woe.
Along the floor walked the worthy fighter
among his thanes—the whole hall thundered—
until he came before the king
and hailed him, asking if he had had

1320   a pleasant night, as he had planned.

Hrothgar spoke, the Shielding's protector:
"Ask not about pleasure. Sorrow is renewed
for the Danish people. Ashere is dead,
the elder brother of Yrmenlaf,
1325   my confidant and advisor in council,
my shoulder companion, with whom I would parry
the blades that threatened to smite our boar-helmets,
protecting each other. As Ashere was,
such a man ought an atheling be!

1330   "A demon wandering in darkness slew him
by night in Heorot, and I know not whither
that creature has borne away her catch,
anticipating feasting. She avenged that fight
of night before last when you laid on Grendel,
1335   grappling him hard, with hostile intent,
when for far too long he had torn and depleted
the folk of my hearth. He fell in battle,
and now there comes to avenge her kinsman
a second mighty slayer of men,
1340   who goes very far in her fury for vengeance
as many a thane may often think
when in great distress he grieves for his treasure-giver,
weeping in his heart. Now that hand lies low
which once gave worthy rewards to you all!

1345 "But there is a tale that the country folk tell,
and hall-councillors, too—I have heard it myself.
They say they have sometimes spotted two
such huge monsters who walk the moors,
wanderers from elsewhere. One was formed,
1350 so far as the most discerning could see,
in a woman's likeness; the second one
shared her exile in the shape of a man,
except he was huger than anyone human!
The folk who dwelt there in olden days
1355 named him Grendel, but nobody knows
his sire, or whether other spirits
were spawned before him.

           "In a secret land
they dwell, among wild fells, wolf-slopes,
windy headlands where a waterfall
1360 hurtles down through the mist into darkness
under the fells. Not far away
in miles lies hidden that lonely mere
overhung by trees covered in hoar-frost,
a deep-rooted wood that shadows the water.
1365 They say every night there appears a strange
fire on the lake!—And no man lives
so wise as to know that water's depth.
Though the stag of the heath, pressed hard by hounds,
should make for the forest with his mighty antlers,
1370 put to flight from afar, he will forfeit his life
on the shore rather than swim in that lake
to protect his head. Not a happy place!
There the wind stirs up sudden storms
where clashing waves ascend to the clouds
1375 and the sky presses down, dark and smothering,
weeping from above.

"Now once more you
alone can save us, but you have never seen
that fearful place where you may find
the surly demon. Seek if you dare!
1380   I shall honor you for taking that on,
just as before, in jewels and gold,
worthy treasures, if you come away."

21. Creatures of the Mere

Beowulf spoke, Edgetheow's son:
"Grieve not, wise ruler! Rather should a man
1385   avenge his friend's murder than mourn him too much.
Death comes to all. Let him who is able
achieve in the world what he wants of glory
and fame among men before he must die—
for the atheling, that is afterwards best!
1390   Arise, great king, let us go quickly
to mark the track of Grendel's mother.
She will not escape under cover, I swear,
to the darkest cavern, or the depths of the sea,
or the wild forest, go where she will!
1395   For a day only endure with patience
the weight of your sorrow—I know you will."
The gray-haired king leapt up, thanking God,
the mighty Sky-Lord, for what that man said.

Then a horse was bridled for Hrothgar,
1400   a stallion with braided mane. In splendor
the king rode, followed by his band on foot
carrying shields. The spoor was clear
as it wound along the path through the woods,
then over the waste land, and onward she had gone
1405   over mirky moorlands, making off
with the corpse of the best of all the comrades
who made their home in Hrothgar's hall.

That son of princes picked his way
over steep cliffs that were loose with stone,
1410   along narrow footpaths and unknown trails,
precipitous mosses where monsters dwelt.
With a certain few he spied out the land,
going before so that others could follow,
when suddenly he came to a stand of trees
1415   bending across gray blocks of stone,
a dismal wood. Dark beneath
lay a stagnant and bloody lake.
To all the Danes it was hard to endure,
a difficult thing for many a thane,
1420   for each of those friends, when on the edge
of that stony cliff they came upon it—
Ashere's head.

                The water welled hotly
as they looked at the lake. Then loud and clear
the war horn sang out, and those walkers found
1425   boulders to sit on, where they could see
many a wondrous serpent winding
through shallows, or lying on rocky ledges—
such creatures of the deep as often, near dawn,
will show themselves to passing ships,
1430   a horrid meeting!

They hurried away,
snapping and angry at the bright sound
of the pealing horn. A prince of the Geats
shot at one of those swimming monsters
so hard with his arrow that the point drove home
1435 to score on its life; then on that lake
he dawdled at swimming, when death was on him!
With a hooked javelin they hemmed him in;
as he bled out his life they thrust a boar-spear
under his scales and drew him to shore,
1440 a wondrous serpent. With awe the warriors
looked on this thing that lived in the mere!

Recklessly Beowulf readied himself
in his coat of mail, carefully woven
and finely adorned, which would dare to enter
1445 that lake; this byrnie would protect his body
so that no malicious monster's claw
could dig in his breast or endanger his life.
And the shining helmet hurling its light
through the depths of that tarn would protect his head;
1450 made worthy with jewels, through the surging waters
the encircling bands would shine as they did
in days long ago, when a great smith wrought it
and set about it the shapes of boars
so that no sharp blade could wound him in battle.

54 1455 And the last helper was not the least.
Hrothgar's *thule** lent it to him—
a hilted sword whose name was *Hrunting*.
Among the highest of inherited treasures,
that iron blade, hardened in blood,

1460 was fretted with serpent-marks; never had it failed
any warrior who wound his fist
hard upon it, in perilous quest
or fierce battle. That was not the first time
that it had to perform a courageous feat!

1465 Indeed, Unferth, the son of Edgelaf,
said little about that strength he had boasted of
earlier at beer, when he lent his blade
to a better warrior; he did not wish
to risk his own life in that turbid lake

1470 with a noble feat. There he lost fame,
renown for courage. Not so the other,
once he had readied himself for war!

22. The Encounter with the Sea-Hag

Beowulf spoke, Edgetheow's son:
"Consider now, great son of Halfdane,

1475 wise leader and gold-friend of warriors,
now that I'm ready, think of those things
we spoke of earlier: if in your service
I should lose my life, you said you would like
to perform the office of father to me.

**thule*: orator

1480 Be, then, a guardian to my band of warriors,
my brave companions, if battle takes me.
And the riches you gave me for honor and glory,
dear Hrothgar, convey them to Hygelac,
so that the lord of the Geats may look

1485 upon that gold and priceless treasure
and know that I found a munificent
giver of rings, who was grateful to me.
Let Unferth have that ancient heirloom,
my wave-marked sword, known widely to men

1490 for its hard blade. With Hrunting I
shall hew myself glory or death shall have me!"
After these words the prince of the Weathergeats
turned away with courage, not caring at all
to wait for an answer. The waters swallowed him.

1495 Part of the day had already passed
before he reached that unfathomed bottom.
At once that ravenous hag who had ruled
those flooding waters for fifty years
discovered, slavering, that some strange human

1500 was diving down to her demon lair.
She grappled with him, gripping him tight
with terrible claws, but she could not harm
his body, for the ring-mail wrapped it around.
Unable to get at the Geat through his sark

1505 or penetrate it with her piercing talons,
the sea-hag, clutching him, swam to the bottom,
dragging that prince to her dismal home
in a manner that, no matter how brave he was,
he could reach no weapon. Harassing him,

1510 many a curious creature of the depths
broke its tusks against his byrnie;
monsters pursued him.

Then the warrior perceived
that now he stood in a strange battle-hall,
where no water was getting him wet

1515 and the swirling tarn could never touch him
because of the roof. He saw ruddy flames,
a blaze of firelight shining brightly.
And then the hero saw that hag,
the incredible mere-witch, and cut a great swathe

1520 through the air with his blade, holding nothing back,
so that crashing on her skull the ring-marked sword
sang out greedily. Then her guest found out
that his gleaming blade would not bite
or harm her, no, that heavy sword

1525 failed him at need. Many a fight
had it endured, often driven
through a fated man's helmet; that time was the first
for that gleaming treasure that its glory faded.

Now Hygelac's nephew, keen for renown,

1530 was resolute; and in a rage
he hurled that sword, with its shining marks
and steel blade, so it struck the ground
and lay there, still. He trusted his strength,
the might of his grip. Thus a man shall do

1535 when he hopes to gain some lasting glory
for his deeds in battle: he does not fear death!

Then by the shoulder Beowulf seized
Grendel's mother—the Geat was now
furious, and had few qualms about fighting—

1540 and swung her, hard, so she smashed to the floor!
Promptly she paid him back for that pass,
closing upon him with a clammy embrace,
and, weary, that strongest of warriors stumbled;
catching his foot, he went crashing down.

1545   She straddled her hall-guest and drew her *sax*,
a gleaming knife; she wanted to get
vengeance for her child. But on his chest
lay the woven sark; that saved his life
with iron rings that blunted both point and blade.
1550   Edgetheow's son would have ended his days
there under the pool, the prince would have perished,
except he was helped by his woven sark,
that hard net of war—and by holy God,
who brought him victory in that battle.
1555   The Ruler of the Skies decided it rightly,
with ease, when Beowulf stood up again.

23. Cleansing the Tarn

He saw before him a fabulous blade
among other armor, an ancient sword
worthy of a warrior, the choicest of weapons—
1560   except it was mightier than any other man
could bear into battle but Beowulf,
heavy and ornate, the handwork of giants.
The daring champion of the Shieldings dived
for that radiant hilt, raised it high,
1565   despairing of his life, lunged angrily,
slashing down hard through the skin of her neck,
breaking the vertebrae, the blade vanishing
through her. Fated, she fell to the floor.
The warrior rejoiced, lifting his weapon.

1570 The flame leapt up and light poured out,
shining as bright as the sun in heaven,
the sky's candle. He cast an eye
around him, then walked along the wall,
holding that weapon high by the hilt
1575 with a single purpose. That sword was still useful
to that prince of warriors, for he wished to repay
Grendel for many a remorseless attack
that the demon had made on the men of the Danes,
more often, by far, than that one occasion
1580 when he had slain Hrothgar's hearth companions
asleep in their beds, and eaten, slavering,
fifteen men of the Danish folk,
and carried another such number away—
hideous booty! Beowulf well
1585 had paid him back, to the point that now
he saw Grendel lifeless, lying on his bed
a foul corpse, as the fight at Heorot
had earlier decreed. That corpse sprang apart
when Beowulf dealt it a final blow,
1590 hacking off Grendel's monstrous head.

At this, the thoughtful thanes who stood
watching by the lake with wise Hrothgar
saw the tarn grow turbulent
and the water bubbling up with blood.
1595 The gray-haired elders spoke together,
saying they did not expect to see
the brave warrior come back again
to hail their king. The water-hag,
many men thought, had murdered him.
1600 So at the ninth hour the noble Shieldings
gave up waiting; the gold-friend of the warriors
turned toward home. But their guests, sick at heart,
sat there, staring at the lake and hoping,
but not expecting, to see their noble
1605 friend once more.

Forming icicles
of iron, that blade, hot with the blood
of monsters, was melting. It soon diminished
entirely, wondrously, like the winter ice
when the Father loosens the bonds of frost,
1610   unwinding the water ropes, he who holds rule
over times and seasons; that is the true God.
The prince of the Weathergeats did not wish
to take more of the treasures (though he saw many there)
than Grendel's head and with it the hilt
1615   adorned with jewels; the damascened blade
had vanished entirely, the venomous blood
of those hideous creatures was that hot!
Then he came away who had accomplished
the fall of those demons, diving up
1620   through the clearing pool; all that expanse
of waters was cleansed when the wandering fiend
passed away from life and this fleeting world.

The leader of the Sea Geats made for land,
swimming bravely, revelling in his booty,
1625   the mighty burden that he had brought with him.
His thanes approached him, thanking God,
glad to see their prince again,
rejoicing that Beowulf was safely back.
They lifted his helmet from his head
1630   and loosened his byrnie. The lake subsided
in low ripples laced with blood.

60 Light-hearted, the men went marching along
  the path which crossed the perilous moor
  to the well-trodden road. Away from the cliff,
1635 bold as kings, they carried that head,
  loathsome to each of those loyal thanes,
  fierce as they were. It took four warriors
  to stagger under the bloody stake
  on which to Heorot they bore that head.
1640 Then all fourteen of them, fierce and brave,
  striding along the stone-paved path,
  suddenly came to the king's bright hall;
  their prince marched with them, proud among his warriors.

  That prince of thanes, well worthy of praise,
1645 brave of deed and destined for glory,
  came inside and saluted the king.
  Behind him by its knotted hair was borne
  that demon's head, where the nobles were drinking—
  monstrous for them and that woman among them
1650 to see, yet a wonder, and they watched it, aghast.

24. The Giant Sword-Hilt

  Beowulf, son of Edgetheow, spoke:
  "O King, this treasure comes from the sea.
  Gladly we give you this golden hilt
  that you gaze on here, for the glory of the Shieldings.
1655 I barely survived with my life that venture
  under the water. It was hard work,
  a battle where I would have been
  taken at once—but God protected me.

In that encounter I could accomplish
1660   nothing with Hrunting, though it is a noble blade;
but the Ruler of Men enabled me
to see hanging, huge on the wall,
this ancient sword (often he aids
one who is friendless), so I drew the weapon
1665   and swung it hard when I had the chance
to kill that demon. Then the damascened blade
melted when immersed in the monsters' blood,
the hottest of battle gore. I took that hilt
away from the foe in fitting vengeance
1670   for wicked deeds, the deaths of the Danes.

"I promise you now that by night in Heorot
you may sleep without sorrow among your warriors;
and, lord of the Shieldings, you need no longer
be afraid, for the folk of your hearth—
1675   that any of the thanes, young or old,
will endanger his life there, as he did before."

Then into the hands of gray-haired Hrothgar
was given the giants' golden hilt,
the ancient artifact. After the fall
1680   of devils, this work of wondersmiths went
to the prince of the Danes—and from this world passed
grim-hearted Grendel, God's adversary,
guilty of murder, and his mother also.
That hilt was kept by the best of kings
1685   who had ever held sway between the two seas,
or dealt out gold in Danish lands.

62   Hrothgar spoke—he looked on the hilt,
      that ancient heirloom. *Upon it was etched*
      the long ago beginnings of strife
1690 *when the fierce giants were slain in the flood.*
      It swept them away, a tribe estranged
      from the Ruler eternal; as retribution
      he sent upon them the surging waters.
      And on that sword-guard, in shining gold,
1695 *graceful runes were correctly engraved,*
      saying for whom that choicest of swords
      had first been made, with its twisted markings
      shaped like serpents. Then the wise king spoke
      (he was Halfdane's son), and all fell silent:

1700 "Of this man let me say, I who administer
      truth and justice throughout our tribe
      as guardian of our people, reflecting on the past—
      that he was well born! Beowulf, my friend,
      before me I see fame, spreading far
1705 through the whole world—yours! Steadily you hold
      your strength with discernment. You will see how I show
      that friendship we spoke of. And to your own folk
      you shall become an abiding comfort,
      a help to your people.

"Heremod was not so

1710 to Edgewela's sons, to the Honor-Shieldings.
He did *not* turn out as the king they needed,
but took to killing his Danish kinsmen,
furiously slaughtering his friends at the table,
his own companions, until in the end

1715 he turned to his death in solitude,
though God had granted him great strength,
exalting him above other men.
But a blood-thirsty mood grew up in his breast,
and from his gold-hoard he gave no rings

1720 to honor the Danes, and he dwelt without gladness,
so that even he suffered distress from that strife—
destroying his kinsmen. Understand from this
the virtue of giving! This advice I offer you
wise from many winters.

                                    "A wonder it is

1725 how mighty God in great generosity
grants discernment to all sorts of men—
and lands, and rank. He rules all things.
At times he allows to wander in delight
the wilful thoughts of a well-born man:

1730 All the joys men can have he has in his hall,
and he holds the trust of protecting his people.
God grants him such power in his part of the world
—a large kingdom—that he cannot, in his lack
of discernment, foresee an end to it.

1735 He lives in luxury, not hindered in the least
by illness or age; no evil sorrow
shadows his heart, no strife anywhere
draws the hateful blade—for him the world
wends to his will. He knows nothing worse . . .

25. "Change Always Comes"

1740   "Until, within him, arrogance
waxes and grows, and the watcher slumbers
who guards the soul; that sleep is too fast,
bound up in cares, and the killer nigh,
waiting to shoot wickedness from his bow.

1745   Then in that man's breast a bitter arrow
strikes under his guard, the sinister promptings
of a spirit accursed. He cannot shield himself.
What he has had for so long now seems too little.
He lusts after gain, and gives no more

1750   the gold rings of honor; he overlooks
even the beginnings of his own glory,
the gifts which God gave him at first.
And in the end it always transpires
that the feeble flesh declines and fails

1755   until fated, it falls. Then someone else
inherits the rings and hands them out recklessly;
he has no qualms about coffers of gold.

    "Shield yourself from conflict with sin,
dear Beowulf, by choosing what is better:

1760   that which endures. Do not be arrogant
now that your power is at its peak—
for a time only, for all too soon
sickness or the blade will snatch your life,
or the fire's assault, or the sweep of the waves,

1765   or brandished sword, or soaring arrow,
or terrible old age . . . or your eye's brightness
will fail and darken, until suddenly death
has overpowered you, noble prince!

"So it was for me. I wielded power
1770   for fifty years, defending the Danes
with spear and sword against assaults
from many a tribe of this middle earth,
so effectively that I knew of no foe
under the heavens. Then look! In my own hall
1775   change came upon me when Grendel appeared,
affliction after feasting when the ancient foe
came on his endless visits to cause me
immeasurable grief. Thanks be to God
that I have lived now long enough
1780   to be able to look at that loathsome head
with my own eyes, at the end of the ancient feud!

"Now, go to your bench, enjoy the banquet
prepared in your honor; we shall pass
much treasure between us by the time morning comes!"
1785   Glad at heart, the Geatish prince
went back at once as the wise king bade
to his place on the bench; and the pleasures of feasting
with those welcome guests began anew
in the hall of the Danes. Shadows darkened
1790   around the warriors. At last all rose,
for the old king with the ashen hair
longed for his bed, and Beowulf, too,
felt an enormous need for rest,
triumphant but weary. At once a hall-thane
1795   courteously offered to accompany him
to the visitors' quarters, and with great devotion
he looked after everything that in those days
a seafaring thane might be thought to need.

1800   The generous hero lay in a hall
that arched high and golden; the guest slept there
until the black raven blithely announced
a joyous daybreak. When the jewel of the sky
thrust back the shadows, the Geatish thanes
were up and ready, anxious to fare
1805   home to their folk. Far was the journey,
and the visitor eager to board his vessel.

Then Beowulf bade that Hrunting be borne
to Unferth; he told him to take back his sword,
an excellent weapon, and that he wanted
1810   to thank him for the loan of a loyal friend
skilled in warfare; in no way did his words
find fault with that weapon. That was a fine warrior!
And then the athelings were anxious to go,
ready in their armor. Honored by the Ring-Danes,
1815   Beowulf walked forward to the raised floor
where Hrothgar was, and he hailed him.

26. Taking Leave

Beowulf spoke, Edgetheow's son:
"We seafarers now have this to say:
having come from afar, we are eager to fare
1820   home to our king. Here we have been
royally entertained; you have treated us well.
If there is any way in this world I may earn
more of your love and esteem, my lord,
by heroic deeds, than I already have,
1825   you need only call me and I shall come.

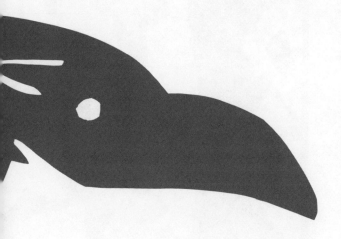

"And if I discover from across the sea
that neighboring tribes are treating you ill
(as monsters did to the Danes for a time),
a thousand or more brave thanes I shall bring
1830   to help at your need. I know that Hygelac,
lord of the Geats and leader of the folk,
young though he is, will urge me on
in words and deeds, to assist you well
as a friend, with esteem and force of weapons,
1835   where you have need of noble warriors.

"If Hrethric himself, as the son of a prince,
determines to go to the home of the Geats,
he will find friends there. Faraway lands
are good to visit, if a man has valor."

1840   Hrothgar spoke to him in answer:
"Wise God himself must send those words
into your heart; I have never heard
a young man speak with more discernment.
You are strong in prowess and in presence of mind
1845   and wise in speech. I consider it likely,
if it comes to pass that a spear pierces
Hrethel's son, Hygelac your prince,
or a blade takes him off in battle, or illness
destroys him, and you are still alive,
1850   the Geats will not find a better friend
than you to choose as their champion and king,
as guardian of their hoard, if you wish to hold
that kingdom of kinsmen.

"Your courage pleases me
better the longer I know you, dear Beowulf;
1855 you have so performed that these two folk,
the Danes and the Geats, shall have peace together
and conflict shall rest, those hostile encounters
and feuds which once afflicted our people.
So long as I guard this land and its coffers,
1860 treasure shall pass between us, fine gifts
of greeting shall cross the gannet's bath.
The craft with twisted prow shall carry
tokens of esteem. I tell you, these people
are disposed to be firm both in feud and friendship,
1865 blameless, according to the customs of old."

Then in that hall Halfdane's son
again gave him treasures, twelve good things,
and said with these gifts he should go home safely
to his own dear kinsmen, but come again soon.
1870 Bending to kiss his friend, the king,
the leader of the Shieldings, laid his hand
on Beowulf's neck. Tears blinded
the gray-haired old man, whose immense wisdom
led him to expect what he wanted least:
1875 that never again would they meet, two gallant
companions in council. The prince was so dear
that Hrothgar could not withhold a sigh,
though as a stern Shielding he shut in his heart
how very much he cared for that man,
1880 locked it in his breast.

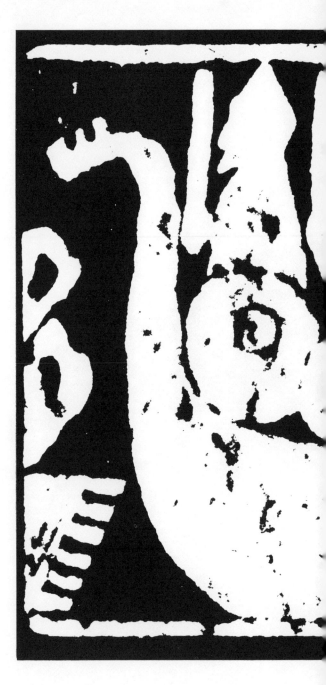

Proudly, Beowulf
strode through the grassy meadows, glittering,
a warrior in gold. His ship awaited
its lordly owner, riding at anchor.
Often on that journey, generous Hrothgar
1885 was acclaimed for his gifts. That was a king!—
blameless entirely, until his strength
was taken by age; it destroys many men.

27. Homeward over the Sea

The brave young Geats came striding together
onto the shore, their ring-mail shining,
1890 hand-woven sarks. The sentinel saw them
approach as before, but felt it improper
rudely to hail such guests from his high
post on the rocks, so he rode down to greet them,
saying how welcome they would seem to their friends
1895 in the handsome byrnies they were wearing home.
Still on the sand, the spacious vessel
with twisted prow was loaded with treasures,
horses and battle-gear. The mast towered high
over Hrothgar's gifts from the Danish hoard.
1900 When Beowulf granted a gilded sword
to the Shielding who had guarded his ship, that man
was accounted a treasure the worthier by his comrades
who drank in the mead-hall.

The land of the Danes
was left behind when they launched their ship
1905   upon the deep waters. Whipping by the mast
was the sail secured by a rope, and the craft
crashed through the waves, impelled by the wind,
swept onward, unhindered, over a sea
that foamed at its prow. Fleetly it crested
1910   wave after wave, until well-known cliffs
of the Geatish shore could be glimpsed from afar,
distant headlands. Then, driven by the breeze,
that gleaming vessel glided ashore.

Down to the harbor that guard came hurrying
1915   who for weeks had been anxiously scanning the waves
for any sign of those sorely-missed travelers.
Securely he anchored their ample ship
with ropes to the shore, lest the raging seas
should carry away that winsome craft.
1920   Then Beowulf commanded that the mighty treasure
be fetched from the hold. Those hardy companions
did not have to go far to find their king,
Hygelac, Hrethel's son, waiting at home
in his fortress by the sea-wall, among his friends.

1925   The building was splendid, the king very bold,
sitting high in his hall, Queen Hygd very young,
but wise and accomplished, though the winters were few
that this daughter of Haereth had dwelt in that castle.
She was never known to be niggardly
1930   in her generous gifts to the Geatish people—

whereas Thryth had been more than miserly
before she became an excellent queen!

None of her friends had dared to face her
except her own lord, or dared to look her
1935 *straight in the eye, but that she would consider him*
ripe for the strangler's rope, drawn tight
by fists around his neck, then followed
by a blade descending on him, poor suspect;
the damascened sword clears up all doubt!
1940 *Such is not a suitable custom*
for a lady to practice, lovely though she be,
for a peace-weaver, killing a man on the pretext
that he has accosted her uncouthly.

Offa stopped that. At ale men told
1945 *of the following consequence: she had become*
far less vindictive and dangerous
from the first moment that she had set foot,
glimmering with gold and the grace of high birth,
on Offa's threshold, thinking to wed him.
1950 *On her father's advice she had ventured the voyage*
over pale green seas to the prince's hall,
and there on the throne, famed for good things,
she well enjoyed both her generous life
and the love in her heart for that lord of heroes,
1955 *for he was accounted, I have heard it said,*
the best and truest between the seas
of all the immense kindred of mankind;
Offa of the spear was widely respected
in gifts and in war. With wisdom he ruled
1960 *over his country, and he fathered Eomer,*
who flourished to be a support to his friends,
but grim in battle, Garmund's grandson!

Brave with his men came Beowulf
striding across the wide sands
1965   of the Geatish shore. From the south was shining
the candle of the world, the sun, as they came
to the fortress where they knew that their noble lord,
the young king Hygelac, a hard man in battle
(who had ordered the slaying of Ongentheow),
1970   was giving out rings. To this ruler the news
of the hero's return was quickly told,
that into the courtyard Beowulf was coming,
bearing his linden shield, alive,
hale from his fight, to the Geatish hall.

1975   At once they made room for the warriors, like guests
in their own home, as Hygelac bade,
and Beowulf, the victor, sat down on the bench
across from his kinsman. In courteous speech
Hygelac welcomed his friend with words
1980   both earnest and hearty, while Hygd the queen
moved through that building with a vessel of mead.
Loving her people, she passed the cup
to each warrior's hand, and in that high hall
the king began to question his friend,
1985   urging him to tell (as curiosity tore at him)
what fine adventures the Sea-Geats had found.

"What befell you, Beowulf my friend,
on that sudden journey that you resolved on,
seeking a fight far over the seas,
1990   a battle in Heorot? Could you help at all
to defeat the sorrow of Hrothgar, that famous
king of the Danes? Because of his grief

I sighed myself, having little desire
that my friend should go, no faith in that venture,
1995   entreating you to leave that monster alone
and to let the South Danes settle for themselves
their war with Grendel. Thanks be to God
that I see you at home now, safe and sound.''

Beowulf spoke, Edgetheow's son:
2000   ''I shall keep no secret, Hygelac my king,
about that battle between us two,
me and Grendel, when we met together
in Hrothgar's hall, that place where he had
formerly caused such cruel sorrow
2005   for all the Shieldings. But I avenged them
so well that in all the world not one
of Grendel's kindred, that greedy race
that dwells in the clutches of malice, has cause
to boast of that fight at midnight. When first
2010   I arrived at that ring-hall to visit its ruler,
he showed me at once (or as soon as he knew
what my purpose was) to a warrior's seat
suitably near to his own son.

''All were high-spirited. Never have I seen
2015   in any hall under Heaven's vault
more pleasure at mead. At times that pledge
of peace to her people, the queen, would pass
among the young men to rally them, making
presents of twisted rings. At times
2020   it was Hrothgar's daughter who handed around
the ale-vessel to each in turn.
I heard those warriors who sat in the hall
call her Freawaru when they thanked her for
some precious gift. She is promised,
2025   fresh and golden, to Froda's son.
It is her father, the Shieldings' friend
and king, who has planned this, counting on it

to settle a painful feud, with the priceless
gift of his daughter. But it is doubtful
2030   that warriors will leave their spears for long
when a prince has fallen, though the bride be fair!

"Little may it please the Heathobards' lord
or his people to see a prince of the Danes
enter their hall with that elegant lady,
2035   *honored by the elders, and on him shining*
an ancient sword, a ring-marked heirloom
a treasure once held by the Heathobards
in the past, when they had the power to keep it . . .

29. - 30. The Fated Hall

"Until they squandered in desperate shield-play
2040   *their own lives and their loved ones' too.*
Then when he sees the ring on that sword
an old spear warrior will speak out,
remembering slayings—his mood is savage—
and grim in his heart will begin to test
2045   *the younger man's courage, recalling him*
to thoughts of war by saying these words:
'My lord, look well upon that weapon.
Is it not the blade your father bore,
glorious in his helmet, gripping it tight,
2050   *wielding it splendidly when the Danes slew him?*
The proud Shieldings won, when Withergyld
lay dying among our fallen men.
Now here the son of one of those slayers
comes jubilant with his jewelled treasure
2055   *into the Heathobards' hall, displaying*
that weapon which you by rights should wear!'

"Thus he incites him, saying such words
at each opportunity, until the time comes
when Freawaru's thane, for his father's deeds,
2060   must fall, blood-drenched from the biting sword,
a forfeit, and the slayer will get away free
with his life, for well he knows his own land.

"Then on both sides the pledge will be broken,
the oath of friendship, when desire for feud
2065   wells up in Ingeld, and after his grief,
cooler will be his love for his queen.
I count the less, then, on loyalty,
sincere friendship without deceit,
from the noble Danes.

                    "Now I shall speak
2070   more about Grendel, so that you may imagine,
O giver of treasures, when we came to grips,
what happened to me. When Heaven's gem
had vanished from the sky, the violent guest
came angry in the evening to seek us out
2075   where as yet unharmed we guarded the hall.
Grim was the fate that befell Handscio
in that sudden battle; the belted warrior
was the first to die. That famous thane
fell prey to Grendel, who gulped him down,
2080   his entire body. But the bloody-toothed slayer
thought only of slaughter, and did not the sooner
want to go out again, empty-handed,
from that high hall. He put out his hand,

2085 eager to test my strength, and took
firm grip on me. A glove hung from him,
gaping and strange, cleverly strengthened
with bands of ornament, adorned all over,
with devilish skill, with dragon pelts.
The wicked ravager wanted to thrust
2090 me in there, guiltless, one of many,
but it dawned on him that he could not do this
when I sprang to my feet in an angry stance.

"It would take too long to tell how I gave
requital to that killer for every crime,
2095 how I, my lord, brought honor to all
the Geatish folk. He got away,
enjoying his life for a little longer,
but he had to relinquish his right hand
to escape from Heorot, and crawl away humbled
2100 to his dismal end in the depths of the mere.

"Well did the friend of the Shieldings reward me
for that hard battle with the brightest treasures
of delicate gold, after day had come
and we had sat down to the warriors' feast.
2105 There were stories and songs. The astute old Shielding
gave us tales from long ago.
At times he stroked the joyous strings
of the round-harp, at times he narrated a story
that was sad and true, or a tale of wonder,
2110 recounted correctly according to custom.
And then, at times, the intrepid old king,
crippled with age, would begin to recall
his former strength, and would heave a sigh
when, ancient of years, he remembered his youth.

2115 "Thus in that hall for the whole day
we took our pleasure, until once more
night came to men. Then Grendel's mother
was ready at once for her wicked revenge.
Sorrowful she came. Her son had been taken
2120 by death—and the war-hate of the Weathergeats.
Vengeful she came, and boldly she killed
a warrior, and life sped away from Ashere,
a wise old councillor of the Shielding clan,
and when morning came they could not carry
2125 their death-weary friend to do him honor
on the funeral pyre with a flaming brand,
for her fiendish embrace had borne away
his body to the depths of the black tarn!

"To Hrothgar that sorrow was the hardest to bear
2130 of all that had fallen upon his folk,
and at his wits' end he asked me once more
(evoking your name) to perform valor,
to put my life at risk in that pool
in a bid for glory and for bright reward.

2135 "As you know, I found that terrible foe,
the witch who guarded those surging waters,
and for a while it was doubtful which
would win, but the water welled with blood
when I hacked off her head in that battle-hall
2140 with an ancient blade. In agony, she
gasped out her last; my own life was still
unmarked by fate, and with many fine things
the warriors' protector acknowledged my worth.

"Thus in accordance with custom lived
2145   the king of the Danes, who gave me no cause
to feel neglect, for he gave me treasures
equal to the honor that I had earned.
To convey them to you, my valiant Hygelac,
was my first wish, to show my good will,
2150   for all my happiness lies in your hands.
I have few close kinsmen but you, my king."

He bade them bring in the boar head-piece,
the helmet of battle, the frost-gray byrnie
and the gleaming sword, and then he spoke:
2155   "That wise king, Hrothgar, rewarded me
with this noble byrnie, but he wanted you to know
the details of whose bright heritage it was.
He said that his elder brother had owned it
and worn it to battle, yet Hrothgar did not wish
2160   to pass it on to his princely son,
proud Heoroward, though he held him dear.
Now all this is yours to use as you will!"

And then I heard that four swift horses,
matched bays of apple brown,
2165   were added to this bounty. Beowulf granted
a huge treasure of horses and war-gear
to his king—and thus should a kinsman do,
not weave nets to trap another,
designing his death in secret. To Hygelac
2170   Beowulf was ever loyal in battle,
and each was thoughtful for the other's welfare.

I heard that he gave to Hygd that necklace,
so wondrously made, that Wealtheow the queen
had given to him, together with three
2175 of the supple steeds in their glorious saddles.
She, too, was more glorious, with that gift on her breast.

Thus Edgetheow's son revealed himself
to be worthy and brave; renowned for his battles,
he aspired to glory. Never did he strike
2180 at a dear companion in a drunken rage,
or know such anger—for he was nourished
by God's own gift, the greatest strength
of all humankind. He was humble as a youth,
and his Geatish comrades had thought him a coward,
2185 nor had the lord of those hearth companions
wished to acknowledge his worth on the mead-bench;
they believed that his spirit was lax and slothful,
unfit for an atheling! But, destined for fame,
the prince saw time reverse such opinion.

2190 Now Hygelac, famous for fighting, commanded
that one of his father's heirlooms be fetched,
a treasure of gold. Among the Geats
no sword was known more noble than this!
He laid it formally in Beowulf's lap
2195 and added to that gift a great estate
of seven thousand hides,* with hall and throne.
They both, in that Geatish realm, had birthright
to land and privilege, but more of the latter
fell to him who was higher of rank.

*A "hide" varies according to time and place; sometimes it is as much as
120 acres. .

Vast were the battles that then developed
in later days, after the death
of Hygelac the king. From behind bright shields
shining swords hewed down his son
Heardred, sought out by invading Swedes
2205   where he stood courageous among his ranks
in the midst of the fray. They had marked him for slaughter.
The broad kingdom came then to Beowulf
who ruled it well for fifty winters
(a noble old guardian of his native land,
2210   wise king to the Geats), until One began—
a dragon!—to rule in the dark of night.

High on the heath he guarded a hoard
inside a stone barrow. Down to it steeply
ran a secret way, and into it wandered
2215   a man who by accident came on that ancient
heathen treasure, and took in his hand
a priceless goblet. Though beguiled by a thief
who came while he slept, the dragon concealed
nothing of his wrath. The neighboring warriors
2220   and farmers found out how great was his fury!

32. Strife Comes Anew

The man had not wished to enter the worm's hoard!
He who performed this fatal act
was a low-born servant in distress,
fleeing from a master's flogging
2225   for some misdeed. He needed shelter
and went inside, but at once he saw
something that made him sick with horror.
Ther was no mistaking the strangeness that lurked
deep in the rock. The wretch was terrified!
2230   Yet still he reached out for more disaster—
and clutched the cup.

of ancient treasure lay in that earth-house.
Once, long ago, a noble warrior
had given the matter grave thought
2235   before he hid that vast inheritance,
dear to his people. Death had taken them,
all but him, at some earlier time,
and left him alone of that lofty race,
a friendless guardian of fabulous wealth.
2240   He felt that his own days would be too few
to enjoy those riches. The barrow stood ready,
newly built above the waves
at the edge of a cliff, with no easy access.
Inside it he carried a kingdom's bounty,
2245   priceless rings and plated gold,
a worthy hoard! Then he said these words:

"Keep, earth, now that kings may not,
this treasure of ours! From you we took it
in the beginning—then grievous strife,
2250   death in battle, took each of my brave
and noble kinsmen who had known such joy
in the gabled hall. Who now remains
to brandish the sword or burnish the cup
that we drank from together? They all have gone.
2255   And from the high crown of the helmet crumble
the plaques of gold; the polishers sleep
who were wont to brighten that mask of battle.
And the cloak of mail that endured the clash
of iron swords biting over the shield—
2260   it rusts on the wearer, no longer a ring-shirt
proud to wander the traveler's ways
by a hero's side. No more will the harp
sing happy songs, nor will the good hawk
swoop through the hall, nor the swift stallion
2265   stamp in the doorway. Death has sent out
many of the living from the land of men!"

82   Thus one man sang his words of woe
        alone, for his lost ones. Sadly he lingered
        days and nights until death's flood
2270   swept over his heart.

                            The hoard was found
        standing open by that old dawn fiend,
        he who burning seeks out barrows,
        the smooth evil dragon who soars through the night
        surrounded by flame, striking fear
2275   into hearts below. He always looks
        for a hoard in a mound, and for many years
        will guard heathen gold. Little good does it do him!
        This time it was for three hundred winters
        he had kept that hoard with a huge craftiness
2280   in its treasure mound, until one man
        humiliated him. That man carried
        the cup to his lord, begging for deliverance
        at his hands from the whip. Thus the hoard was exposed,
        the treasure diminished, when mercy was given
2285   to the churl, empty-handed, for his lord was enchanted
        by this golden vessel of long ago—

        Then the dragon awoke and strife came anew!
        He snaked along that surface of stone
        and found a footprint. The foe had stepped
2290   all too close to his evil head.

Thus may a man not marked by fate
survive with ease many a venture
by the grace of God! But the hoard's guardian
moved along eagerly, hoping to meet
2295   the thief who had sorely disturbed his sleep.
Blazing with wrath, he blasted around
outside the barrow; no one could be seen
in all that waste. But the thought of war
had stirred him up, and at times he struck inward,
2300   seeking his cup, and he saw again
how someone had tampered with his treasure,
disturbed his gold. That guardian waited
impatiently for the day to pass;
by the time night fell his fury was boundless!
2305   He wished to pay back with a billow of flame
his dear cup's theft. Day drew to a close
as the dragon wished, and he did not wait,
lingering on that cliff ledge, but leapt up with fire,
a coil of flame! A cruel beginning
2310   that was to the folk. Far worse was the end:
they paid for that gold with their giver of rings.

The fiend began to spit out flame,
to burn the bright buildings, pouring from above
a stream of fire that men fled from, aghast—
2315   that hostile sky-worm sought to leave
nothing alive. The leaping fury
of his wicked malice was widely seen,
how he hunted and hated the Geatish folk,
intent on harm. Then back to his hoard,
2320   to his secret den, he would shoot before daybreak,
having fanged those people about with fire,
with peaks of flame. He put his trust
in his home to protect him—that hope proved false!

The horrible news was quickly made known
2325   to Beowulf, that in burning flames
his home, the best of halls, had perished,
the gift-throne of the Geats. That brought the gravest
despair to his heart, the heaviest thoughts,
for he feared that he might have offended God,
2330   bitterly angered him, possibly broken
some ancient law. With a long sigh,
he mulled over such dark imaginings—
as was not his custom. The coiling dragon
had destroyed from outside that island of safety,
2335   the people's fortress, with fire; for that
the prince of the Weathergeats planned revenge.
The protector of warriors, the lord of the troop,
commanded his smith to make of iron
an ornate shield, for well he knew
2340   that a shield of wood could offer no shelter
against flame. That good old atheling,
who for years had held the wealth of the hoard,
was doomed to encounter the end of his days
in this fleeting life, along with the dragon.

The prince of rings despised absolutely
the thought of advancing with all his thanes
in a great force seeking a solitary flyer;
he did not fear his fight with the dragon
or take much account of that creature's strength,
for he had braved many great battles,
passing safely through difficult straits
from the day that he, alone, had cleansed Heorot
and crushed to death the demon strength
of that loathsome clan.

Nor was that the least
of his encounters where Hygelac was killed,
the princely friend of the Geatish people,
Hrethel's son, slain on Frisian soil
by a blood-thirsty sword in a mighty battle,
beaten down by the blade. Beowulf survived
that slaughter by means of his skill in swimming,
taking with him thirty trophies
when he launched himself alone on the sea.
Of little value were the Hetwares' victory
taunts at Beowulf as they bore down
with their wooden shields, for few there were
who left him, able to limp back home!

After that battle Edgetheow's son
swam to his people across the sea.
There Hygd offered him hoard and kingdom,
rings and throne, for she did not think
that her noble son could hold the ancestral
hall against strangers when Hygelac was dead.

But even in need the thanes could not
find any means of persuading that man
2375 to be high king over Heardred's head,
the son of his lord, or to rule his land.
Instead, he supported the young prince
among the folk with friendly advice
until he was older. Then two exiles
2380 sought Heardred out, the sons of Ohtere
rebelling against his brother, Onla,
the best of kings who gave kindly treasures
betokening honor between the two seas,
a famous prince. That was fatal to Heardred.
2385 For hospitality, Hygelac's son
received a mortal blow from the sword.
Then Onla left for his own land
when Heardred lay dead, and he allowed
Beowulf to hold that royal hall
2390 and rule the Geats. That was a good king!

34. The Father's Lament

But Beowulf did not forget that battle,
the fall of his lord, in later days,
when Eadgils, the other son, sought his aid.
He helped him with an army, with warriors and weapons,
2395 across the wide ocean. Then Eadgils avenged
his cold exile: he slew his king!

Thus valiantly Beowulf had survived
battles and feuds and bitter fights,
each dangerous quest, until that day
2400   when he had to confront the fiery worm.
The ruler of the Geats strode forth in rage,
one man among twelve, to seek that monster.
He had found by then the reason for that feud,
the baleful slaughter, for someone had brought
2405   the fabulous cup to the hands of his king,
and he who had wakened the hideous strife
now made in that troop the thirteenth man,
a fearful captive. Trembling, he was forced
to show the way, and he went unwilling
2410   to where he alone knew the earth-hall lay,
the underground barrow, close to the ocean,
the pounding waves. Wondrous ornaments
filled it within, and a frightful custodian,
primed for war, held those precious things
2415   beneath the earth. That treasure was not
an easy bargain for anyone to get!

The king sat down at the top of the cliff
and turned to face the friends from his hearth.
The heart of the lord of the Geats was heavy,
2420   his mind restless and ready for the slaughter,
wyrd very near, waiting to seek
his soul's hoard, and to wrest asunder
his life from his body. Not for long now
would that warrior's life be wound with flesh!

2425   Beowulf spoke, Edgetheow's son:
"I endured in my youth many dangerous battles,
violent encounters; I recall them well.
I was only seven when I was received
by Hrethel, the ring-lord, from my father's hand.

2430   *He cared for me and treated me kindly*
with gold and feasting, a friendly kinsman.
I was not any less beloved to him
in his athelings' hall than his own sons,
Herebald and Hathcyn and my dear Hygelac.

         "Untimely prepared for that eldest prince
2435   *was the bed of death by a kinsman's deed,*
when Hathcyn struck down Herebald
with a bright arrow from his horn-tipped bow:
he missed his mark and murdered his kinsman,

2440   *shot his own brother with a bloody dart—*
unaccountably, a sorrowful crime
that could not be paid for, painful to the heart,
a valiant life that must go unavenged,
a miserable thing—as for an old man

2445   *who can only stand by when his boy is riding*
young on the gallows, and a grieving lament
is all he can say, for his own son hangs there
as food for the ravens, and old and infirm
he cannot offer any help at all.

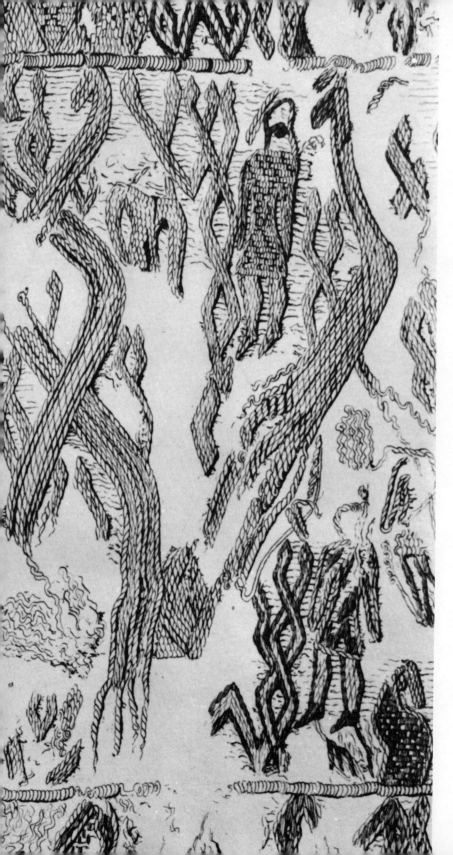

2450   "Then every morning reminds him again
      of his boy's dying, and he does not wish for
      another son who will guard the ancestral
      hall and fortune, when the first has been
      exposed to death through some evil deed.
2455   Sadly he sees in his son's dwelling place
      a wine-hall empty—the wind has ceased—
      a round-harp bereft—the rhythms sleep—
      a hale youth in darkness. There is no harp-thrum there,
      no songs in the wine-courts as once there were.—

35. Beowulf's Attack

2460   "Then he goes to his couch and begins to chant,
      alone, for his lost one. All too large
      seem house and lands.

                             "Such was the heaviness
      the lord of the Geats felt after the loss
      of his son; he could not right that slaughter
2465   by punishment, or even permit
      the relief to himself of hating the slayer
      for his violent deed, though he was not dear to him.
      That sorrow weighed so sorely upon him
      that he gave up life's joys, and chose God's light.
2470   But he gave to his sons, as a good man does,
      his landed wealth, when he passed away.

For this unorthodox interpretation of lines 2456-57, see *Neophilologus* 62
(1978), pp. 442-446.

"Then again there was war between the Weathergeats
and the Swedish folk across the sea—
hard battles after Hrethel died.
2475   Ongentheow's men were mighty and bold,
active warriors, who did not want
to sue for peace, but at Sorrowhill
fell on the Geats and slaughtered them fiercely.
My kinsmen were valiant; they avenged all that
2480   by strenuous fighting, and I have found
that the Swedish leader bought his life
at a high price. But to Hathcyn, now king
of the Weathergeats, that war proved fatal.
I recall that Hygelac avenged Hathcyn.
2485   A blade struck down his brother's slayer;
though Ongentheow launched an attack upon Eofor,
the Geat split open the old Scylfing's
masked helmet. His hand remembered
many a battle, and did not hold back
2490   the killing blow.

                              "I, too, requited
the gifts of my prince, as was most proper,
with my bright sword on that battle field;
he had given me the holdings and the hall I was born in.
He had no reason to seek a courageous
2495   man of less might from among the Gifthas
or the Danes of the Spear, or the Swedes themselves,
to buy loyalty there, for keen was my longing
to stand with my king in every conflict,
to show my love so long as this sword
2500   endures, which so often has given me aid;
it fell to me in my fight with Dayraven,
the Huga, whom I slew with my bare hands.
He did not manage to bring to his master
that bright adornment, the Danish necklace,

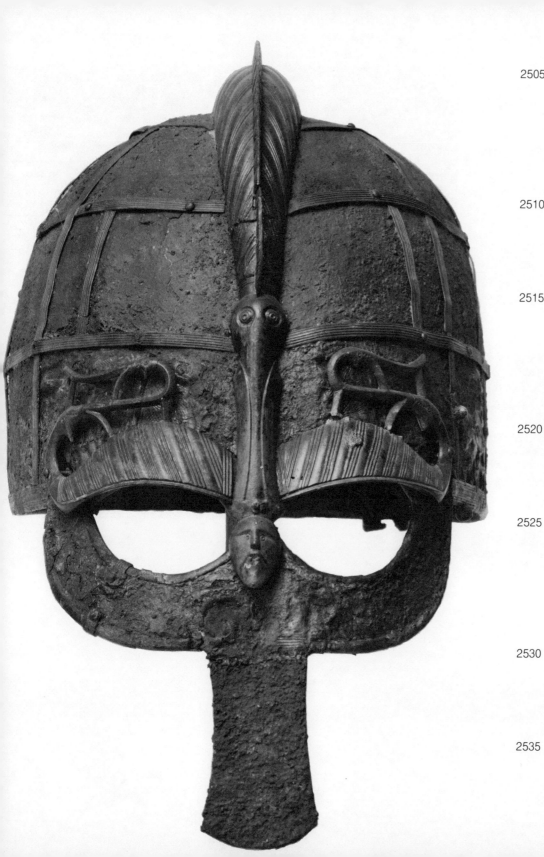

2505 *from Hygelac's body, for in that battle*
he fell, bearer of the Frisian standard—
and not by the sword; beneath my grip
his body broke. But now the blade
that shines in my hand shall fight for this hoard!''

2510 In brave words Beowulf vowed
his last deed: "I have endured
many a battle, yet again I must,
as wise guardian of the Geats, seek conflict
with that murderous dragon, if he dares
2515 to come to me out from his earthen hall."

Then final words he spoke to his friends,
standing there masked in their shining helmets:
"I would bear no sword or weapon to that battle
if I knew another way to fight that worm,
2520 to carry out my boast with honor
and come to grips, as I did with Grendel.
But this time I fear hot battle fumes,
dragon breath and deadly venom,
so I'll fight the beast with shield and byrnie,
2525 and I shall not flee a foot's space
from that barrow's guardian. But what *wyrd,* and God,
decree, will happen. My spirits are high,
and I need no boast to inspire me now.

"Wait here above, my byrnied warriors,
2530 shining in your armor, to see which of us shall
better survive this violent quarrel
down on the cliff side; and remember, this quest
is not within anyone else's power
but mine alone, to match him in strength
2535 and quell him nobly. With courage I shall
gain that gold, or grim will be
the defeat that claims the life of your friend!"

Helmeted and fierce, the brave fighter
rose with his shield; in his shining byrnie,
2540 trusting in his solitary strength, he went
clambering down the stones, no cowardly man!
Then he who had ventured on violent battles,
when manly virtue had counted for much
in the clash of tribesmen, came upon
2545 an arch of stone standing in the wall
through which a fiery stream came flowing
out from the mound, nor could any brave man
pass without burning to penetrate
deep to that hoard through that dragon flame.

2550 Then the Weathergeat let a single word
burst out in fury from his breast;
stout-hearted, he stormed, and through the gray stone
that bright and vivid voice resounded.
Hate was awakened! When the hoard's guardian
2555 heard human speech, there remained no space
to ask for friendship, for billowing forth
from beneath the gray stone came noxious smoke
from the monster's hot breath. The barrow thundered!
On the cliff's ledge the Geatish lord
2560 swung his shield to face that stranger.
This fired the heart of the fearsome serpent
with battle fury. Already Beowulf
had drawn his sword, an heirloom shining
with tempered edges. Terror came
2565 raging at each enemy from the other!

The prince took his stand behind his steep
and curving shield, as the dragon coiled
abruptly together. Beowulf waited.
The gleaming worm came at him; gliding
2570 smooth in its flames, it sped to its fate.
But the time that Beowulf's shield protected
his life and limb was less than he hoped for

when first he had thought of having it forged
to wield in that battle—for *wyrd* did not
2575 decree him victory. But his valiant hand
had swung the sword, and down it struck,
so hard against those gleaming scales
that the bright edge blunted against the bone.
It bit less nobly than its king had need of
2580 in such bitter straits!

                      Then the barrow's guardian,
enraged after that ferocious swing,
spat out flames that billowed far
around the battle. Beowulf did not
boast of his victory, for his naked blade,
2585 that weapon so long a willing companion,
had failed him at need. That famous son
of Edgetheow did not find his journey easy
when it came to leaving the land of his kinsmen:
against his wishes he would have to go
2590 to a dwelling elsewhere—as all are doomed
to take their leave of this fleeting life.

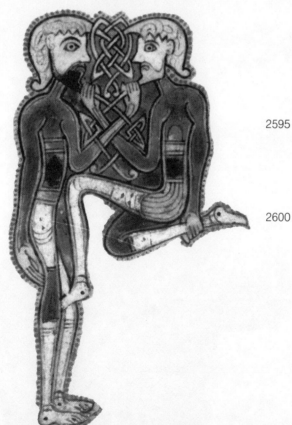

Then again those enemies clashed together.
The guardian of the hoard took heart, his breast
swelling with rage, and the erstwhile ruler
2595 found himself trapped in the heart of the fire!
Not at all did those champions so carefully chosen
from his comrades leap up to stand by their leader,
valiant in the fight, no, they fled to the woods
to save their lives—except one, whose sorrow
2600 tore at his heart. The ties of kinship
can never be ignored by a noble man!

He was called Wiglaf, Weohstan's son,
a beloved shield warrior, a Shilfing prince
of Swedish kindred. He saw that his king
2605   was suffering from the heat beneath his helmet,
and recalling those good things he had granted him—
the wealthy home of the Wagmunding clan
and every folk right his father had owned—
he could not restrain himself from stretching
2610   for his lindenwood shield and his lambent sword.

That sword was famous to folk as the heirloom
of Eanmund the Swede, Ohtere's son
who was slain as he stood on Geatish soil,
killed by Weohstan. To his Shilfing kinsman
2615   *Weohstan took those battle trophies,*
helmet and byrnie and ancient blade,
and Onla granted him Eanmund's gear,
his nephew's armor, saying nothing
about the slaying of his brother's son.
2620   *For many years Weohstan kept that weapon*
and the byrnie, bright treasures, until his son
could perform such deeds as his father did.
Then among the Weathergeats Weohstan gave him
that priceless war-gear when he passed away,
2625   *a wise old fighter.*

This was the first time
that the young champion had had a chance
to stand in battle beside his lord.
His courage did not fail, nor his father's heirloom
falter at that fighting, as the fiend discovered
2630   later, when they came to clash together.

Wiglaf spoke, saying many words
of censure to his friends. His heart was sad:
"I remember that time, drinking our mead
in the lofty hall, when we promised our lord
2635 who was giving us weapons of gold to engage us,
that we would repay him for that precious gear
if need occurred, requite him in action
for helmet and sword. Such was the reason
that we were the men whom he chose from his warriors
2640 for this venture, remembering our vaunted worth
at the giving of weapons. He had thought we were
eager to wear helmets and hurl our spears.
Our lord had planned to do this alone;
the protector of the Geats undertook it without us,
2645 he who had gained the greatest glory
among men for his deeds, but the day has come
that Beowulf needs the combined strength
of all his warriors.

                        "Let us go to his aid,
and help our leader lapped round by that heat,
2650 by those grim flames! God knows
that I should prefer the fire to devour
my body with my lord than to live without helping him!
A shameful thing if we bore home shields
after this fight, unless we first
2655 had felled the foe to save our friend,
our generous prince. It is not a just
return for his bounty that alone of the band
he should suffer affliction, and fall in battle.
For myself, I shall share my shield and helmet,
2660 byrnie and sword with Beowulf!"

As he waded then in his shining war-gear
through the deadly smoke, he said to his lord:
"My king and kinsman, this is your calling.
In the days of your youth you swore that you
2665 would never give up your noble purpose
so long as you lived! My lord, single-minded,
you must now try to protect your life
with all your might. I shall help you!"

After those words, the angry worm
2670 launched his attack for a second time.
Brilliant and shining in sheets of flame
and waves of fire he sought his foes,
burning Wiglaf's shield to the boss!
Not even his byrnie could offer him aid,
2675 so the brave youth dived beneath his dear
kinsman's iron shield, when his own
was gone in the blaze. Then again the king
remembered valor, and swung his mighty
blade with great strength, so it struck down hard
2680 on the beast's head—and broke apart!

Nagling was the name of that noble sword,
but it failed at battle. Beowulf was not granted
success with any blade of iron;
his hand was too strong. No sword could help him.
2685 They tell me his swing would overtax
the mightiest blade when he brandished it,
and in battle he was none the better for it.

Then to the attack for the third time
rushed the fierce fire-drake, intent on his feud,
2690 charging at that hero when he saw his chance,
raging with fire, gripping him around
the neck with his terrible fangs! And now
Beowulf's life-blood drenched his body!

Then at need, I heard, Wiglaf made known
2695   at his king's side his strength and courage,
the hardy keenness that was his heritage.
He did not heed that dragon's head
but burnt his hand in helping his kinsman,
striking a little lower down
2700   so that his sword went slicing into
that fearsome beast, and the billowing flames
began to diminish. Then the lord of the Geats
came to his senses, remembered the *sax*
beneath his mail, and drawing that knife,
2705   plunged the blade in the dragon's belly!
They felled the beast; combining their strength,
the two noble kinsmen had cut him down
both together. Thus should a man be,
a thane at need!

                              To Beowulf that
2710   marked the last of his mortal victories,
of his deeds in this world, for that wound the dragon
had given him began to grow,
to fester and burn, and soon he found
that within his breast a bitter poison
2715   was welling up. The old warrior
sat down to think (and deep were his thoughts)
on a seat by the wall, observing how the work
of giants, great arches of jutting stone,
supported that ancient place with pillars.

2720 Then with cool water gentle Wiglaf
begin to refresh his failing lord,
to lave away the blood, and loosen
the helmet from that weary head.
Beowulf spoke, despite the pain

2725 of his dreadful wound, for he knew full well
that he had played out his allotted portion
of pleasure on earth; that was all passed away,
and death had come incalculably near:

"Now I would give my battle gear

2730 to my heir, had I been granted any
son of my flesh to safeguard my memory
beyond my life. For fifty years
I have kept these people safe; no king
dwells among neighboring tribes who dares

2735 to seek me out with brandished swords
and terrify us. In my time I abided
what fate would bring, held fast to my own,
sought no strife nor swore unrightfully
vows unkept. Because of all this

2740 I take pleasure, even now in pain from my wounds,
that the Ruler of Men has little reason
to accuse me of the murder of kinsmen
when life leaves my body.

"Now quickly, go look
at the hoard that is stacked beneath that gray stone,

2745 now that the dragon lies dead, dear Wiglaf,
sorely wounded, bereft of his wealth.
Hurry, so that I may have the time
to admire that treasure, that mound of gold
and ruddy jewels, and then the more gently

2750 in sight of that brilliance I may abandon
the life and lordship I have held for so long."

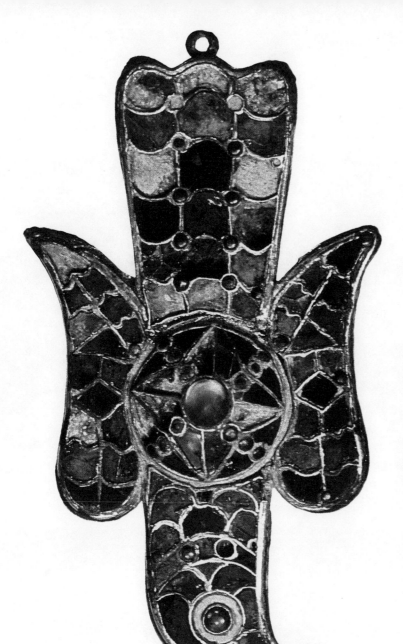

I heard that Wiglaf, Weohstan's son,
on hearing these words of his wounded lord,
obeyed him, and went in his ring-mail byrnie,
2755 woven for battle, into that barrow.
There the young prince, as he passed along
the bench, saw many a jewelled brooch,
and gold things glittering all over the ground,
wondrous weapons hanging high on the wall
2760 in the den of that dragon, the old dawn flyer,
and drinking goblets, their polishers gone,
sockets agape where garnets had been,
and helmets rusty with age, and rings
twisted with cunning. Easily may treasure,
2765 gold in a mound, overpower the mind
of anyone human, heed it who will!

He also saw hovering, high over the hoard,
a golden banner, the greatest of woven
wonders, and from it a light poured forth,
2770 showing him further along the floor
the glowing wealth. But no glimpse of the dragon
was there to be seen, for the sword had destroyed him.

Then those riches, I heard, were ransacked by
one man alone, who laid in his arms
2775 all that he wished of that giant-wrought wealth,
goblets and dishes, and the golden banner,
that brightest of beacons. The old lord's blade
with its edges of iron had earlier slain
him who had guarded those heaps of gold
2780 for a long time with the terror of fire
hot before the mound, surging up murderously
at the darkest hour—until he died.

Wiglaf was in the wildest haste
to get back with the treasures, tormented by
2785   the question of whether he would come upon
his prince alive, the Weathergeats' lord
whom he had left dying for his deed of courage.
Bearing that fabulous wealth, he found
his leader bloody, that life at the ebb.
2790   Then Wiglaf, once more, caressed him with water
to soothe him, until the spear of his words
burst through his breast, and Beowulf spoke,
in pain, looking upon the gold:

"For all this magnificence I must needs
2795   give words of thanks to the wise Lord,
eternal God, for this gold I see,
for letting me gain such a gift of wealth
for my dear people before my death!
I have traded my life for these splendid treasures;
2800   they will fulfill the needs of the folk—
I, their lord, may be here no longer.
After the pyre ask them to build me
a mound shining above the shore
at Whalesness, high and whitely gleaming,
2805   to remember me by, and for seafaring men
to speak of as Beowulf's barrow, whenever
they see it from a distance when driving their ships
on the misty paths of the perilous seas."

That bold leader then lifted from his neck
2810   his golden necklace, and gave it to Wiglaf
with his blade and byrnie and the brilliant helmet,
and commanded the youth to use them well:
"You are the last of our Wagmunding line;
wyrd has lured all the others away,
2815   my courageous kinsmen, called to the death
of athelings, and I must go after them!"

Those were the last words from the old lord's
heart, before having to taste the hostile
flames of the pyre, but his soul went forth
2820   to find the judgment of the just.

39. Wiglaf's Words

Sick at heart the young man saw
his dearest friend painfully faring
beyond his reach, stretched there on a rock
at the end of life. The slayer, also,
2825   lay there dying; that terrible dragon
was curved like a bow, though bent no longer
to hold the guardianship of the hoard
in wicked bitterness, for the blade had deposed him.
That hammer's legacy, hard and sharp,
2830   had cut him down in his coiling attack,
and now he lay dead near the barrow door—
no more to arch through the still air of midnight,
to float through the heavens flaunting his riches,
a sight to remember!—for he sank to earth,
2835   a sky-demon quelled by the strength of that hand.
Indeed, I have heard that rare is the hero
(though he were daring in every deed)
who would not have failed in such a feat—
braving the venom of dragon breath
2840   or running his hands through that golden hoard,
if he came upon its fiery keeper
awake in the cave! To Beowulf was
a king's ransom of gold requited;
but man and monster had met the end
2845   of this fleeting life.

It was not long then
before the traitors slunk out from the trees,
all ten together, having broken their troth,
not daring to acknowledge their lord's great need
for their spears in battle. Bright in their armor,
2850 but shamefully bearing their shields, they came
forward to the place where their prince lay dead,
and regarded Wiglaf. Wearily he sat,
as a comrade should, near his lord's shoulder,
trying to revive him, to no avail.
2855 Much as he cared to, he could not manage
to keep life burning in the breast of his king,
nor move the Lord's will in any manner,
for God in justice and judgment had ordered
the day and its deeds, as he always does.

2860 And then from Wiglaf those craven warriors
found rough words ready for their return!
Thus he spoke, the son of Weohstan,
sadly to those friends he had formerly loved:
"This must be told, for it is the truth.
2865 Beowulf gave you gold and byrnies for battle,
the warriors' armor you are wearing now.
When on the mead-bench you sat making merry,
he would pass a helmet to a hall companion,
or a byrnie, or whatever he could find that was beautiful
2870 from home or afar to honor his friends—
a loyalty that was completely lost,
thrown away on thanes like you!

"When war came upon him, the king of our people
had no cause to boast of his battle companions!
2875 Yet the God of Victories helped him avenge
his life by his own hand when high deeds were needed.
And I, in my own way, tried to offer
protection at battle, indeed attempted
to persevere beyond my power,

2880 and the deadly foe seemed the feebler for it.
After I struck him, the flames less strongly
flowed from his jaws. But defenders too few
stood by our king when strife came upon him.

"Now giving of treasure to honor your troth
2885 must end, and your kinsmen, because of you,
must lose their right to enjoy this land
and the comfort of living among loyal friends,
when the athelings hear how men will harken
far and wide to your defection,
2890 your inglorious deed. Death is better
to every warrior than life without honor!"

40. Hygelac's Arrogance

He ordered then that the outcome of the fight
be announced above, where the shield-bearing nobles
had sat, sad in mind, all morning, all day,
2895 waiting, expecting one of two things:
the return of their lord, or the last day
of his dear life. Little did that man
who rode up to the headland hide his news;
his voice rang out with all the truth:

2900 "Now gone is our joy, our generous prince!
The lord of the Geats lies on his deathbed,
stretched out in slaughter by the serpent's deed!
Endlong beside him his enemy lies
slain by the *sax*. With the sword our king
2905 could find no way of wounding that monster,
the wicked destroyer. Now Wiglaf, the son
of Weohstan, sits in watch over Beowulf,
one man beside his friend who is slain,
keeping guard with a grieving heart
2910 over friend's head and foe's.

"Now our people may find
that the time has come for an era of trouble,
when the Franks and the Frisians hear of the fall
of our strong king. Hard was the strife
destined for the Hugas when Hygelac's fleet
2915   of proud ships sailed for Frisian shores;
the Hetwares repelled him with superior might
and brought it about that the king in his byrnie
should not survive to divide his loot
with his fighting men, but fell among them!
2920   Since that victory, the Merovingian
king of the Franks has denied us all kindness.

"Nor do I expect we can count on peace
or good faith from the Swedes, for when Ongentheow slew
Hathcyn, the son of Hrethel, in battle
2925   at Ravenswood, it was widely known
that arrogance had prompted the Geatish people
to join in that feud of the Shilfing folk.
They had launched an attack upon Ongentheow's troops,
but fiercely he had returned their foray,
2930   cut down the ruler of the Geats, and rescued
his lady, Onla and Ohtere's mother,
a gaunt old woman stripped of her gold.
Grimly he pursued his Geatish foes,
but they found a refuge in Ravenswood
2935   (with difficulty, for their leader was dead).

"Then the king surrounded those wretched few
whom the sword had left, and promised them sorrow
all night long, saying when the light
of day revealed them, vengeful blades
2940   would hack down some, while others would hang
high on the gallows as a game for the crows!
But dawn brought help and relief; they heard
the sound of Hygelac's well-known horn,
his trumpet of war, as hot on their tracks
2945   their lord came to save his beleaguered band.

"Then the bloody swathe of the Swedes and the Geats,
the track of their slaughter, was readily seen,
how they stirred up feud and strife between them.
Wise old Ongentheow went with his kinsmen,
2950 *grimly, to seek the safety of his fortress,*
a good stronghold on higher ground.
He had heard much of Hygelac's valor
and did not have faith in his own defences—
that he had the power to parry the attack
2955 *of the Geats, or to save the Swedes' bright gold,*
or their women and children. So in Ravenswood he went
to seek his refuge. But the Geats pursued
the Swedes, and Hygelac's banners were seen
flashing victoriously over the fields
2960 *when his men pressed forward to harry that fortress.*

"There the silver-haired king of the Swedes
was brought to bay with a shining blade,
and that mighty ruler had to submit
to the angry judgment of Eofor the thane.
2965 *Wulf, his brother, had struck the old warrior*
so fiercely that the blood jetted forth from the veins
under his hair. But the old Shilfing,
never afraid, with a far more vicious
onslaught, had quickly requited that thrust
2970 *in the time it took him to turn around.*
Then Wulf was unable to raise his weapon
to repay the old king for the powerful blow
that had cut right through the crest of his helmet.
He began to waver, wet with blood,
2975 *and dropped to his knees—but he was not doomed yet!*
He recovered in the end, though the wound nearly killed him.
Eofor the brave, seeing his brother
lying still on the ground, raised high his sword,
a jewelled weapon wrought by giants,
2980 *and struck past his shield at that Shilfing helmet*
across from him, killing the king of the Swedes!

"At last the Geats turned to attend their fallen.
They raised up those wounded who were able to walk,
and took them to join in the jubilant victory.
2985 *Eofor the thane took King Ongentheow's*
royal byrnie, robbing him also
of hilted sword and shining helmet;
he bore these accoutrements of the king
to his prince, Hygelac, who promised him
2990 *fitting reward among the warriors.*

"He did as he said; Hrethel's son
acknowledged that battle with noble treasures
when they all came home. To Wulf and Eofor
he granted homesteads of a hundred thousand
2995 *hides of land, and a hoard of rings.*
No one could blame him, they had been so brave.
Then he gave to Eofor his only daughter
as wife, to grace a worthy dwelling.

"That is the feud and the conflict of foes,
3000 *the enmity of thanes, that leads me to think*
that the men of Sweden will seek us out
when they hear of Beowulf's latest battle—
how that hero has fallen, who formerly held
our hoard and kingdom against the hatred
3005 *of vengeful lords, a valiant leader*
who honored his warriors, and altogether
behaved nobly!

"Now haste is best.
Let us go to look on the king of the Geats,
and carry our giver of golden rings
3010 to his lofty pyre. What burns with our lord
shall not be meager, for there is the mighty
hoard of gold so grimly bought,
and paid for at last with his own life,
fabulous treasures. The flames must devour them,
3015 the fire embrace them, with none held back
to be worn by a warrior, or a beautiful woman
who graces her neck with a gleaming jewel.
Sad must she go, bereft of gold,
to pace, alone, down alien paths,
3020 now that our lord has passed beyond laughter,
harp song and happiness. Now shall the hand
of the warrior on many cold mornings grasp
for his ashen spear; not at all shall singing
rouse him from dreams, but the dark raven,
3025 eager for thanes, will call out many things,
asking the eagle how well he ate
when with the cruel wolf he plundered corpses!"

Many and true were the terrible things
that messenger said; not much did he gild
3030 his facts or words. Then the warriors,
with grief-stricken faces, rose to their feet
to see the harrowing sight at Eaglesness.
On a sandy ledge of the cliff they saw,
lying on his deathbed, the lord who once
3035 had given them rings; now he had reached
the end of his life. But the lord of battles,
that warrior of the Geats, died a wondrous death!—
for also they beheld, hard by their king,
the amazing creature whom he had killed,
3040 his mortal foe. That huge fire-drake,
a horrible monster scorched black with the heat
of his own flames, lay fifty feet long,

stretched out on the sand. By night he had sprung
in joy to the skies, then sailed back down
3045   to seek his den. He was now quite dead,
never more to coil in his earthy cave.

Nearby stood cups and beautiful goblets;
plates lay there, and precious swords
eaten through by rust. For a thousand winters
3050   they had been buried in the bosom of the earth.
Once that mighty hoard had been woven
around with a spell, so that its splendor
could not be disturbed by anyone tampering
with all its gold, unless God himself,
3055   the High King of Victories, revealed the power
of opening the hoard to whom he wanted,
to whatever man seemed meet to him.

42. The Rifling of the Hoard

Clearly the dragon was doomed to fail
in wickedly trying to keep the treasure
3060   hidden in darkness! Indeed, that guardian
struck down his foe, but that feud was well
and quickly avenged.

                    Where the man of valor
shall meet his death as ordained by fate
is always a mystery, when he may no longer
3065   live with his kinsmen in the lofty hall.
So it was for Beowulf, when ready for battle
he approached the mound. How his departure
from the world would occur, he could not foresee.
Those long-ago princes who placed that treasure
3070   in the ground until doomsday had cursed it grimly,
saying that he would be guilty of sin,
bound by the worship of wicked idols,
tormented by greed, who touched that gold.
(*He* was not wracked by gold-fever. Rather
3075   had he wished it granted by the owner's good will!)

Wiglaf spoke, the son of Weohstan:
"Often the will of one man brings
exile to many, as it does to us.
We could not persuade our noble king,
3080   protector of the Geats, to take our advice
not to meet that guardian of the mound,
but to let him lie where he had for so long,
dwelling in his lair until the world's last days.
But Beowulf held to his high destiny,
3085   and the hoard is won. That *wyrd* was too harsh
that prompted thither the prince of our land!

"When it was granted that I might go
inside that barrow and see all around,
an entrance by no means easily won
3090   to that earthen house, in haste I took

as much with my hands as I could hold,
and bore that burden of brilliant treasure
outside to my king. He was still alive then,
wise and aware, an old man wearily
3095   speaking in sorrow. He wished me to say
farewell, and to bid you to build a mound
where the pyre was, as high as his deeds were heroic,
a beacon as great as of men he had been
the worthiest of warriors in all the world,
3100   so long as he had been granted life
for the giving of rings.

                              "Now let us go
to gaze once more on the gold in the mound,
at those shining treasures. I will show you the way,
so that you may have the joy of beholding
3105   that abundant wealth. Let the bier be made ready
quickly, by the time that we have returned,
so that we can carry our beloved king,
our dear prince, to the place where he
must rest in the keeping of the High Ruler."

3110   That brave young warrior, Weohstan's son,
commanded those nobles to announce to others,
to hall-lords and fighters, that they should fetch
wood for the pyre and bring it to the place
where the king would lie. "For the leaping flame
3115   now must devour the noblest of men,
who has often stood in a shower of iron,
a blizzard of arrows impelled by the bow
over the shield-wall, feather-clad shafts
obediently aiding the flight of the barb."

3120   Carefully, then, Wiglaf culled
seven of the best from Beowulf's band
of Geatish thanes, and in gleaming armor
the eight warriors went together
beneath that dark roof. Wiglaf raised
3125   a flaming torch as he went in front.
Lots were not cast for whom should carry
that gold away, now that no guardian
gave any thought to those precious things
that were left in the mound. Little did those men
3130   who heaped up the treasure so hastily
have scruples at fetching it out! And the fire-drake—
they shoved him over the cliff, let the shining
waves enfold him, take him away!
They loaded a wagon with all the wealth
3135   of countless treasures, and carried their lord,
their white-haired king, to Whalesness.

The Geatish people prepared for him
a huge pyre high on the headland,
splendidly hung with helmets and shields
3140   and shining byrnies, as he had bidden.
The lamenting warriors then laid their lord,
their mighty prince, in the midst thereof,
and a few were assigned to set alight
that fire on the cliff top. A cloud of woodsmoke
3145   rose up dark from the roaring flame
encircled with weeping—the wind subsided—
until the blaze had broken that bone-house,
hot within.

                          Sad at heart,
the last companions mourned for their prince,
3150   and a woman with her hair bound up bewailed
the passing of Beowulf. In a song of despair
and suffering, she told of sorrows to come,
of how she feared greatly days of grief,
many a raid of ravaging warriors,
3155   the shame of slavery. Heaven swallowed the smoke.

Then they raised for the ruler of the Weathergeats
a mound on the hilltop, high and broad,
to be seen from afar by seafaring men,
a warrior's beacon, built in ten days.
3160   Around the ashes of that atheling
they set an enclosure so fairly designed
that the wisest men should find it worthy,
and they placed in the mound the precious treasure
of rings and jewels from the ravaged hoard,

3165   the twisted gold they had taken earlier.
They let the earth hold that princely hoard,
left it in the ground, where still it lies,
as useless to men as it was of yore.

Then around the barrow rode the bravest
3170   of the sons of athelings, twelve in all,
expressing their sorrow and mourning their prince,
wishing to declare what that warrior was like.
They chanted of his courage, acclaiming his deeds
and his generous manhood—as it is meet
3175   that a man should salute his lord in words
and love him in his heart, when at last he must
go forth from his failing cloak of flesh.

And thus the Geatish people grieved
at the death of their prince: his hearth companions
3180   said that he was, of the world's rulers,
the kindest of men and the gentlest of kings,
the most loving to his people, the most longing for esteem.

Appendices for
BEOWULF

The Finnsburg Fragment

Though this battle poem is called a fragment, it is probably very nearly complete, with only a few lines missing at the beginning and the end. It is technically a "heroic lay," and concerns an event which is seen from a more humane and thoughtful perspective by the *Beowulf* poet (lines 1068–1159). One can learn a great deal about the style of *Beowulf* by comparing the two treatments.

It is also of great interest to readers of *Beowulf* to have independent accounts of historic or traditional events that are mentioned in the poem. As the history in *Beowulf* is continental, most of the sources by which we can confirm it are Scandinavian or Latin. But the "Finnsburg Fragment" is an Old English poem (existing only in George Hickes's 1705 transcription, as the manuscript was lost); it tells us of an event in Frisia which is already a historic tale when related in sixth-century Heorot. If it commemorates a fifth-century battle in Frisia, the Hengest of the fragment and episode may well be the same Hengist who, according to the Anglo-Saxon historian Bede, led his Germanic mercenaries to Britain in 449, first to aid the British king Vortigern and then to oust him.

The hero of the fragment is not the warrior Hengest but his young leader, the Danish prince Hnaef. As Hnaef is still alive here, whereas the episode in *Beowulf* begins with the scene of his sister Hildeburh mourning his and her son's deaths, the fragment must precede the episode in the order of events. The two contending forces are the Danes, in the guest hall, and the Frisians, outside. The fragmentary opening is usually thought to be a question asked by one of the Danes when he sees a flash in the darkness outside, though it can also be read as part of a statement.

"... Horns aflame?"
Then Hnaef began chanting, young chieftain in war:
"No dawn is this rising, nor a dragon flying,
nor is it the horns of this hall aflame—
5 it is them, bearing arms at us! Birds cry out,
the wild wolf howls, the war-spear roars,
shield answers shaft! Now shines the moon
wandering in the clouds. Now deeds of woe
rise to perform the strife of this folk.
10 Therefore, awake now, warriors mine!
Hold high your shields, think hard of courage,
turn to the battle, bear yourselves bravely!"

Rose many a gold-armored thane, then, girding on weapons.
To one door strode the splendid warriors
15 Sigeferth and Eaha, swinging their swords,
and to the other went Ordlaf and Guthlaf,
and Hengest himself came hard in their tracks.

Outside, Guthere was pleading with Garulf
not to fight in that first attack
20 or flaunt his armor before those doors,
for fierce was the warrior who wished to take it.

But high and clear keen young Garulf
hurled his question: who held those doors?
"My name is Sigeferth," said he, "of the Sedgas,
25 a prince well known for experienced warfare.
For you the outcome is already certain,
which fate you will choose, if you challenge me!"

Then a roar of slaughter arose in that building.
Shields held high by the warriors were shattered,
30 bone-helmets burst, the hall-floor boomed,
until at that fight Garulf fell,
the first of those dwelling in Finn's land,
Guthlaf's son. And good men around him
fell as corpses where the raven flew
35 black and shining. Sword-light blazed
as though all Finnsburg were on fire!

Never have I heard of warriors more worthy,
of sixty who bore themselves better in battle
or gave more in return for shining mead,
40 than those young heroes did to Hnaef.
They fought five days, and not a man fell
of that hardy band, and they held the doors.
At last, wounded, a warrior lay dying.
He said that his battle-shirt had been broken,
45 that hardest of byrnies, and his helmet pierced too.
Then at once the leader of those warriors asked
how others were bearing up under their wounds,
or which of the young men . . .

Later in the fight Hnaef himself is slain. His place as leader of the Danish party is taken by Hengest, who eventually must agree to a truce with the Frisians when neither side has the force to continue fighting.

BEOWULF:
A Reconstructed Chronology
of Events

The poet gives us Beowulf's three great fights in a chronological sequence which provides the basic linear organization of the poem. Interwoven between these fights, however, occur many references to Scandinavian feuds, which add historical authenticity but are not presented chronologically. As this distorted sequence of unfamiliar events in ancient Scandinavia is one of the most difficult barriers for the modern reader of *Beowulf* to overcome, I offer the following reconstruction for easy reference.

This chart is based on Klaeber's reconstruction, especially p. xlv. As he admits, the only date verifiable by outside evidence is Hygelac's death ca. 521 (now thought by some to have taken place in 524); the other dates, calculated from Hygelac's death, are guesses based on legends, contemporary accounts, and archaeological finds. Beowulf and Wiglaf (but not Wiglaf's father Weohstan, O. N. Véstein) represent the only family group mentioned below whose existence is not in some way confirmed by evidence outside the poem. Bracketed dates place *Beowulf* in a larger and more English historical context; these events are not referred to in the poem.

Key to tribes

D	*Danes*
F	*Frisians*
G	*Geats*
HB	*Heathobards*
S	*Swedes*

[449]	[Bede's date: Hengist and Horsa come to Vortigern's aid in Britain.]
495 G, S(?)	Beowulf born, son of Edgetheow (a Swede?), grandson of the Geatish king Hrethel on his mother's side.
498 HB, D	Froda kills Halfdane of the Danes; Froda's son Ingeld born.
499 HB, D	Heorogar, Hrothgar, and Halga (Danes) kill Froda.
502 G	Hathcyn accidentally kills his brother Herebeald.
503 G	Their father King Hrethel dies of grief, and Hathcyn becomes king of the Geats.
503 G, S	Swedes attack Geats at Sorrowhill: FIRST SWEDISH-GEATISH FEUD begins.
510 G, S	Hathcyn and Hygelac attack the Swedes and abduct their queen. In the ensuing BATTLE OF RAVENSWOOD both Hathcyn of the Geats and Ongentheow, the Swedish king, are killed. Hathcyn's brother Hygelac becomes king of the Geats and Ohthere king of the Swedes.
515 G, D	*Beowulf kills Grendel and Grendel's Mother*
[518]	[According to the tenth-century *Annales Cambriae*, Artorius (King Arthur?) wins an important battle at Mt. Badon.]
518 HB, D	Hrothgar, who with his brothers Heorogar and Halga had killed King Froda in vengeance for their father's death, gives his daughter Freawaru in a "peace-weaving" marriage to Froda's son Ingeld to forestall a renewal of the feud.
520 HB, D	Ingeld attacks after all, burns down Heorot, but is then

defeated by Hrothgar and Hrothulf (according to the poem *Widsith*).

524 G, F — Hygelac of the Geats is killed in his ill-fated Frisian raid; Beowulf escapes by swimming, after killing Dayraven.

524 G — Hardred, Hygelac's son, becomes king of the Geats with Beowulf acting as regent.

525 D — Hrothgar dies; his nephew Hrothulf comes to (usurps?) the throne. (Hrothulf, of dubious morality in *Beowulf*, is the great hero-king Hrolf Kraki in Icelandic saga.)

532 G, S — SECOND SWEDISH-GEATISH FEUD begins.

533 G, S — Death of the Swedish king Ohtere (Ottar Vendel-Crow, buried at Vendel in Uppland, Sweden). His brother Onla seizes the throne, while his sons Eanmund and Eadgils seek refuge in the Geatish court. Onla attacks the Geats, kills their young king Hardred; Beowulf (by Onla's permission?) becomes king of the Geats. In the battle Eanmund is killed by Weohstan, Onla's champion. Weohstan is the father of Wiglaf, who is Beowulf's only surviving relative and his most loyal companion. (Eadgils' desire to avenge his brother's death, a family feud rather than an element in the national wars, would cause his enmity not only toward Weohstan but, in case of Weohstan's death, toward his son Wiglaf as well—and if Wiglaf becomes king of the Geats after Beowulf this could serve as an excuse for the Swedes to attack yet again.)

535 G, S — Beowulf supports Eadgils in war against Onla.

575 S — Eadgils is laid in a mound at Old Uppsala.

583 G — This date is a poetic fiction: note the date of Beowulf's birth. *Beowulf dies in battle with a fire dragon.* Wiglaf probably succeeds him as king of the Geats. (THIRD SWEDISH-GEATISH FEUD begins? Flight of the survivors abroad?)

[625] — [A cenotaph ship containing rich treasures analogous to those described in *Beowulf* is buried in a mound at Sutton Hoo in East Anglia.]

[800?] — [A masked helmet is lost at Coppergate, in York, rediscovered in 1982.]

[750–1035?] — [An English poet, at sometime during the Anglo-Saxon period, composes *Beowulf*, about a Scandinavian hero.]

Names in
BEOWULF

Numbers in parentheses refer to lines of the poem.

Abel (107). Adam's son in *Genesis*, slain by his brother Cain.

Ashere (1323, 1329, 1422, 2122). Hrothgar's warrior and friend, slain by Grendel's mother.

Beowulf (19, 54). The son of Shield Shefing, a Danish king, whose name is given as "Beow" in genealogies outside the poem. Not the hero of the poem.

Beowulf (207, 343, and passim). The hero of the poem. His name, spelled *Biowulf* in the second part of the manuscript, means "bee-wolf," which may be a kenning (standard metaphor) for "bear."

Breca (506, 517, 524, 532, 583). Beowulf's competitor in a youthful swimming match; he later became a ruler of the Brondings.

Brondings (521). Tribal name; see entry for **Breca.**

Brosings (1199). Tribal name; the owners of a famous necklace, the Brosinga mene ("necklace of the Brosings"). This name recalls the Brisingamene, Freya's necklace in the *Elder Edda*.

Cain (106, 109, 1261). Emended from *Beowulf* manuscript *cames* and *camp*, this is the name of Adam's elder son in Genesis, slayer of his brother Abel.

Danes (1 and passim). Tribal name; the inhabitants of Denmark, ruled over by Hrothgar in the time of the poem. Also called "Spear-Danes," "Bright-Danes," "Ring-Danes," "North-, South-, East-, and West-Danes," "Shieldings" (the kindred of Shield), "Honor-Shieldings."

Dayraven (2501). A Huga warrior whom Beowulf slays, possibly to avenge the slaying of Hygelac, his king.

Eadgils (2393, 2395). A son of the Swedish king, Ohtere, supported in battle against Onla by Hardred, king of the Geats after Hygelac's death.

Eaglesness (3032). The site of the dragon's lair, a Geatish headland.

Eanmund (2612, 2617). A Swedish prince, Eadgils's brother (see entry above), slain by Wiglaf's father, Weohstan, in the second Swedish-Geatish feud (ca. 533).

Edgelaf (499, 590, 980, 1465). Unferth's father, a Dane.

Edgetheow (263 and passim). Beowulf's father, probably a Wagmunding.

Edgewela (1710). Referred to only once as a Danish ancestor, otherwise unknown.

Eofor (2486, 2964, 2977, 2986, 2993, 2997). The Geatish slayer of King Ongentheow of the Swedes. The name means "boar."

Eomer (1960). Son of the Angle king Offa. A tyrannical figure in Germanic literature.

Eormenric (1201). A historical king of the East Goths (died ca. 375 A.D.)

Finn (1068, 1081, 1128, 1147, 1150, 1156). The king of the East Frisians, at whose stronghold the "Finnsburg episode" and "The Fight at Finnsburg" take place.

Finnmark (580). The land where Beowulf comes ashore in his swimming match with Breca "is usually identified with Finnmarken in the north of Norway" (Klaeber), the land of the Finnish Lapps.

Fitela (880, 889). The nephew of Sigemund in *Beowulf*, nephew (and son) of Sigurd in Old Norse sources; the name is cognate with the second element of Old Norse Sinfjótli.

Franks (1210, 2912, 2921). Tribal name, etymon of modern "French."

Freawaru (2023). Hrothgar's daughter, betrothed to Ingeld of the Heathobards to settle a feud (see **Froda** below).

Frisians (1094, 1207, 2506, 2912, 2915). Tribal name; inhabitants of what is now part of the Netherlands.

Frisian land (1126, 2357). Frisian slaughter (1070). See entry above.

Froda (2025). King of the Heathobards, the father of Ingeld; slain by Hrothgar of the Danes.

Garmund (1962). Father of Offa, king of the Angles.

Geats (194 and passim). Tribal name; Beowulf's people, the inhabitants of what is now southern Sweden. They are also called the "Sea-Geats," "Weather-Geats," "Battle-Geats," the "Hrethlings," etc.

Gifthas (2495). Tribal name; the inhabitants of a district north of the lower Danube in what is now Germany. They were dispersed by the Lombards in the sixth century.

Grendel (102 and passim). The monster slain by Beowulf in Hrothgar's hall; according to the poet, of the kindred of Cain (lines 1265–66).

Guthlaf (1148). A warrior of the Danish contingent at Finnsburg.

Haereth (1928). The father of Queen Hygd, wife of the Geatish king Hygelac.

Halga (61). A Danish prince, the younger brother of Hrothgar and the father of Hrothulf.

Hama (1198). A character occurring in Middle High German epic and Norse saga, a friend turned enemy of Eormenric (see entry above).

Halfdane (57 and passim in kinship formulas). A king of the Danes, Hrothgar's father.

Handscio (2076). A Geatish warrior slain by Grendel.

Hardred (2204, 2375, 2388). Hygelac's son, who becomes king of the Geats after Hygelac's death.

Hathcyn (2434, 2436, 2482, 2924). A Geatish prince, Hygelac's elder brother (see entry for *Herebald*).

Heathobards (2032, 2037). Tribal name; the people of Froda and Ingeld.

Heatholaf (460). A Wylfing warrior slain by Beowulf's father.

Heatho-Raemes (519). Tribal name; a tribe living in southern Norway, where Breca came to shore in his swimming match with Beowulf.

Helmings (620). Tribal name; Wealtheow's people.

Hengest (1083, 1091, 1096, 1127). Leader of the Halfdanes after Hnaef's death at Finnsburg; possibly the warrior to whom Bede refers as Hengist (see *Jutes*).

Heorogar (61, 468). Hrothgar's elder brother, a prince of the Shieldings.

Heorot (78, 166, 403, 432, 593, 766, 991, 1017, 1177, 1267, 1278, 1279, 1302, 1331, 1587, 1671, 1990, 2099). The great hall of the Danes built by Hrothgar, probably corresponding to the royal dwelling at Hleithr (Leire) in Norse tradition. The Old English name means "Hart."

Heoroward (2161). Heorogar's son, a Danish prince mentioned only here.

Herebald (2436). A Geatish prince, Hygelac's eldest brother, slain accidentally by his brother Hathcyn, much as Baldur the Beautiful was slain by Höth in Norse myth (the names are notably similar).

Heremod (901, 1709). A king of the Danes who slays his companions at the table; an exemplary type of the king who goes wrong.

Hetware (2363, 2916). Tribal name; the Frankish inhabitants of the lower Rhine.

Hildeburh (1071, 1114). King Finn's Danish wife, who sees her son and her brother slain on opposing sides at Finnsburg.

Hnaef (1069, 1115). A prince of the Halfdanes, Hildeburh's brother.

Hoc (1076). A ruler of the Halfdanes, father of Hnaef and Hildeburh.

Hrethel (374, 453, 1847, 1923, 2357, 2429, 2474, 2924, 2991). A king of the Geats, Hygelac's father and Beowulf's grandfather.

Hrethric (1189, 1836). A Danish prince, one of Hrothgar's two sons (probably the elder).

Hrothgar (61 and passim). The king of the Danes who established Heorot.

Hrothmund (1189). A Danish prince, probably the younger of Hrothgar's sons.

Hrothulf (1181). Hrothgar's nephew, the son of his brother Halga; a great king in Norse saga literature, where he is known as Hrolf Kraki, but of dubious character in *Beowulf*.

Hrunting (1457, 1490, 1660, 1807). Unferth's sword, which he lent to Beowulf for use against Grendel's mother.

Hugas (2502, 2914). Tribal name; the Franks.

Hunlafing (1143). A warrior of the Danish contingent at Finnsburg.

Hygd (1926, 2172, 2369). Hygelac's wife, queen of the Geats.

Hygelac (195 and passim). The king of the Geats, Beowulf's lord.

Ingeld (2065). The son of Froda, betrothed to Hrothgar's daughter Freawaru to settle the Heathobard-Danish feud. (See *Froda* above).

Ingwine (1043). Tribal name; the Danes ("Ing's friends").

Jutes (902, 1072, 1088, 1141, 1145). Tribal name. In my view, the *Eotenas* of *Beowulf* are the Jutes, a contingent of whom Hengist led to England in 449 A.D. according to Bede's *Historia Ecclesiastica*. A case has been made recently, however, for translating the word, which also means "giants," simply as "enemies" where it occurs in *Beowulf*.

Merovingian (2920). The king of the (Merovingian) Franks.

Nagling (2681). Beowulf's sword, which he uses unsuccessfully against the dragon.

Offa (1944, 1949, 1958). A historical king of the continental Angles.

Ohtere (2380, 2612, 2931). A historical king of the Swedes, the son of Ongentheow.

Onla (Old English Onela, Old Norse Ali) (62, 2381, 2387, 2617, 2931). A historical king of the Swedes, son of Ongentheow; foe of Hrolf Kraki (Hrothulf) in *Hrolf Kraki's Saga*.

Ongentheow (Old Norse Angantyr) (1969, 2475, 2486, 2923, 2928, 2949, 2985). A historical king of the Swedes.

Oslaf (1148). One of Hengest's Danish warriors at Finnsburg.

Ravenswood (Old English Hrefnawudu, Hrefnesholt) (2925, 2937). A forest in Sweden where a major battle in the Geatish-Swedish wars takes place.

Shefing (4). Patronymic of Shield, "first" king of Denmark.

Shield (4, 18, 26). The mythical king of Denmark celebrated in the first 52 lines of *Beowulf*.

Shieldings (30 and passim). Tribal name; the Danes, or "followers of Shield."

Shilfings (2487, 2603, 2927, 2967, 2980). Tribal name; the Swedes, the Swedish dynasty.

Sigemund (876, 881, 884). The son of Waels (Old Norse Vólsungr), who in *Beowulf* performs the deeds of Sigurd the dragonslayer in Norse literature.

Sorrowhill (Old English Hreosnabeorh) (2477). The Geatish site of a major battle in the Swedish-Geatish wars.

Swedes, Swedish (see also Shilfings) (63 and passim). Tribal name, inhabitants of the east central part of what is now modern Sweden. (See **Geats**.)

Swerting (1202). Hygelac's grandfather, a Geat.

Thryth (1931). A type of the evil queen, who reformed when she married Offa of the Angles.

Unferth (MS Hunferth) (499, 503, 530, 1165, 1465, 1488). Hrothgar's "thule" or official orator.

Wagmundings (2607, 2813). Tribal name; the kinship group to which Wiglaf and Beowulf both belong.

Waels (877, 896). Sigemund's father.

Wayland (454). The famous smith of Germanic legend, mentioned also in other Old English poems.

Wealtheow (612, 665, 1162, 1216, 2173). Hrothgar's wife, queen of the Danes. (The name, meaning "foreign" or "Celtic" "captive," has led some to suggest that she might be British.)

Weathergeats (Old English Wederas, Weder-Geatas). See **Geats**.

Weathermark (298). The land of the "Weather-Geats." The name-element *weather* suggests "storm," and the name is closely analogous to "Wuthering Heights."

Wendels (348). Tribal name; probably the Vandals, or the inhabitants of Vendel in Uppland, Sweden, or of Vendill in North Jutland.

Weohstan (2602, 2614, 2620, 2623, 2752, 2862, 2907, 3076, 3110). Wiglaf's father, a Swedish follower of Onla.

Whalesness (2804, 3136). A promontory on the Geatish coast where Beowulf's barrow was built.

Wiglaf (2602, 2631, 2673, 2694, 2730, 2745, 2752, 2783, 2790, 2810, 2852, 2860, 2906, 3076, 3120). Beowulf's only surviving kinsman, "the last of the Wagmundings," and the only warrior who stands by him in the dragon fight.

Withergyld (2051). A Heathobard warrior slain by a Dane.

Wulf (2965, 2971, 2993). A Geatish warrior wounded by Ongentheow of the Swedes. (See **Eofor**).

Wulfgar (348, 360). A prince of the Wendels, serving as an official at Hrothgar's court.

Wylfings (461, 471). Tribal name; the tribe antagonized by Beowulf's father when he slew Heatholaf.

Yrmenlaf (1324). A Dane, younger brother of Ashere.

On Translating
BEOWULF

Beowulf is an intensely social poem. Beowulf the hero fights in succession three monsters who threaten the hall of fellowship, where treasures and courtly words are exchanged at the feast. The two isolated Grendel-kind threaten the community of the hall; the dragon in his miserliness threatens the very principle of exchange and giving. The form of the poetry in which this story is told is as communal as the content, a part of the ritual of hall-telling far older than any words we have on paper. I have tried to approximate that form as closely as I could, to capture the ancient "music" of the poem, so long as it does not impede the flow of the story itself.

In an Anglo-Saxon hall, the alliterative stressed meter, the densely packed diction, and a formal delivery heightened the language of poetry and distinguished it from prose—and also made it memorable when poetry was entirely an oral art. In this translation I have attempted to imitate the meter. Not long ago translators were adamant that imitative meter was out of the question for Modern English. Henry Cecil Wyld went so far as to say, "Attempts to reproduce the rhythm of the old meter and to preserve its regular alliteration have produced a form that cannot give pleasure to modern readers. Alliteration . . . cannot properly be insisted upon as an essential of the verse." But such brilliant modern poets as Basil Bunting in Northern England and more recently John Peck in America have been rehabilitating that meter for us. I believe that today it can be insisted on, if delicately controlled, and that it must be insisted upon, if the translator intends to offer any true impression of the nature of Anglo-Saxon poetry. Just as the deeper preoccupations of the society are mirrored in the monster-killing story of *Beowulf*, so are the stylized traditions of that society reflected in the surface structure of the poem.

The Meter

The Old English verse line, usually printed in two separate half-lines in the editions, normally contains four beats or stresses, with two stresses and at least one alliteration in each half-line. The third stress of the four-stress line is called the head stave because it always carries the alliteration, as in these two lines:

> 1785 G̲lád at heárt, the G̲éatish prince
>   went báck at ónce as the w̲íse king báde . . .

Glad alliterates with *Geatish*, the third stressed word of the line, and *once* alliterates with *wise*. From this we see that the sound is significant, not the alphabetical letter, for *o* alliterates with *w*. *Went* does not carry the metrical alliteration because it is not stressed. In this second line there is additional alliteration on the *b*'s of the first and fourth stresses, a feature that occurs in the original at points of narrative importance, such as the first line of the poem: "we g̲árdéna in ge̲árdágum." In this line the main alliteration is on *g*, occurring in the head stave, the third stressed syllable, and there is also secondary alliteration on *d*. In the Old English verse line the head stave may alliterate with either of the two previous stressed syllables, or with both, but not with the last; in formal Anglo-Saxon versification, to alliterate with the same sound on both head stave and fourth stressed syllable would be a mistake.

In my translation I have not been so rigid; I frequently alliterate not on the head stave but on the last stressed syllable, as throughout the following passage:

2688 Then to the attack for the third time
rushed the fierce fire-drake, intent on his feud,
charging at that hero when he saw the chance,
raging with fire, gripping him around
the neck with his terrible fangs. And now
Beowulf's life-blood drenched his body.

On the whole, alliteration on the final stressed syllable is a heavy rhetorical technique that is best reserved for intense or exciting passages, like this, where the content can absorb it.

My principle for representing the metrical form of the poem is to produce a four-stress line with at least one alliteration connecting the first two stresses with the last two. But I have adopted various stratagems and emphasized others that are used in Old English in order to tone down the force of this feature for modern ears. For example, I may alliterate on an internal syllable, as on two of the lines above: at*t*ack and *t*ime, 2688, and *r*aging and a*r*ound, 2691. Or I may alliterate on a syllable of relatively lesser stress, as in the second line below:

1776   . . . . when the ancient foe
cáme on his éndless vísits to cáuse me
immeasurable grief.

Here alliterative *came* is one of the four stressed syllables in line 1777, but it receives less emphasis than does non-alliterating *endless* (which is linked through assonance with *ancient* and *immeasurable*). Similarly, in line 1759 the alliteration is subdued syntactically:

1758 Shield yourself from conflict with sin,
dear Beowulf, by choosing what is better.

Here the word Beowulf contains the stressed syllable alliterating with *better*, but is deemphasized by being in a parenthetical clause. In the first line above, 1758, the alliteration is on *sh* and *s*; this is not acceptable in Old English prosody, though alliteration between one vowel and any other, strangely enough, is:

758 No wise man among the Shieldings
had ever expected that anyone
could break that beautiful antlered building.

In addition to muting the alliteration by such methods as these, I have used other expedients such as breaking the rhythm, usually by relocating the caesura as in lines 2692 and 1759 above, or by proceeding from many syllables in one half line to very few in the following. So long as the four stress rhythm is maintained, the number of syllables in a line is variable.

King Alfred says in the preface to his translation of Gregory's *Pastoral Rule* that he translated sometimes word by word and other times meaning by meaning; any translator works to some degree by "meaningful mouthfuls." While working in phrasal units, I have tried specifically to keep the integrity and sequence of the half line intact. This is not always possible to do if one's first aim is to preserve the sense; the minimal liberty, which I have sometimes taken, is simply to reverse half lines for syntactic clarity.

I have preserved the drafts of my work on a single line which proved more difficult to translate into alliterative meter than I anticipated. A review of these drafts will demonstrate both my procedure and the sort of difficulty I encountered. The line did not seem to offer particular problems:

2706 Feond gefyldan—ferh ellen wræc

This may be literally translated:

"The fiend they felled—life courage conquered."

Dropping "fiend," since "dragon" was immediately antecedent in line 2705, I began with this outline translation using Klaeber's vocabulary gloss on *ellen*. Usually such a trial run with a list of synonyms occurred only in my head; I actually put this one down on paper in order to see more clearly what I was doing:

                                        courage
They felled him, ——ing his life with (their) valor
                                        strength
                                        zeal

My first attempt at a verse line was:

They felled him, destroying his life with their strength.

This line "gallops" metrically, but I felt it would be acceptable if surrounded by more static lines. The pair *destroying* and *strength* contains nice alliteration on *str*, an alliteration which moreover links the two concepts across the half lines. But in this context the connotation of *strength* is incorrect. It is Wiglaf's and Beowulf's *zeal* that has overcome the dragon, or even more precisely their courage-in-kinship. The poet makes a point of this. So I tried:

They felled him, destroying his life with their spirit.

Spirit is an acceptable synonym for *zeal*, but in proximity to *life* the nuance is again inaccurate, taking on through association a spirituality which is certainly not in the original. My next attempt was:

They felled him, overcoming his life with their courage.

But technically one "overcomes" one's enemy, not his life. So I varied it once more, using now Klaeber's alternative gloss on *wræc* in this context, "drove out," to change the verb:

They felled him, deprived him of life with their pluck.

This is obviously the sort of translation one avoids at all costs; though again the meaning is "correct" in dictionary terms, the associations of the word *pluck* turn the achievement of these heroes into a Hardy Boys' adventure. But *prowess*, containing the sense of heroic achievement and excellence as well as of courage, has precisely the connotation needed here. Beowulf—

2705   plunged his blade in the dragon's belly.
They felled him, deprived him of life with their prowess,
the two kinsmen, cutting him down
both together. Thus should a man be,
a thane at need.

With this I sat back, very pleased with my achievement. For a minute. Then with horror I saw what I had done, or rather what the hazards of language had outrageously done to my translation: "Felled" by those kinsmen who had "cut him down," the dragon had turned into a tree!

I took a break to clear my head, and began again. Professor Robinson has observed in his introduction, "Translation is the art of taking as few losses as possible in a losing battle." I finally settled on:

They felled the beast; combining their strength,
the two noble kinsmen had cut him down
both together . . .

Perhaps as many losses as gains even with this version. Until writing this essay I had not noticed the amazingly obvious intrusion of Shakespeare into line 2707. He is the most difficult of all English poets to keep out.

It will be obvious from this example that the choice of word is, if not precisely dictated, certainly modified by the verse form. How much the Anglo-Saxon poet was controlled by his verse is a matter of debate among scholars. As a practicing poet my opinion is this: *always* there is an appropriate word available to fit your structure and your meaning if you "dowse" for it long enough and are patient and dedicated enough. Old English is more limited in vocabulary than Modern English in some respects, more liberal in others; just as Eskimo is notable for its many words for kinds of snow, so is Old English for its many poetic terms for warriors and the sea. The translator into modern English is limited by our lack of synonyms in these areas, but in other areas has more resources on which to draw than the original poet had. I think it balances out.

But there is one important resource the translator does not have that the poet did, and that is a "high-context culture" in which the communal audience would share backgrounds and assumptions. In addition to the meter and delivery, which would immediately mark the words being uttered as the high rhetoric of poetry, there are a number of rhetorical devices the audience would expect and respond to, devices such as variation, ironic understatement, word play, echo and envelope patterns, and dramatic retardation, among others. I comment on some of these in the notes. Here I want to discuss one particular pattern of diction native to the verse form and familiar to the hall-audience: the oral formula.

The oral formula is a recurrent syntactical pattern in which the elements may vary: "Unferth spoke, the son of Edgelaf" (499), "Beowulf spoke, the son of Edgetheow" (529). Such phrases have been described in terms of Anglo-Saxon jewelry as filigrees of gold into which the poet could lay at will the gems from his word-hoard; the gems were his own, the filigree into which they were laid was manufactured by tradition. Formulas are of many patterns. Another one recurrent in *Beowulf* is "That was (adjective) (noun)," often used climactically. It first appears in *Beowulf* in the description of Shield Shefing: *þæt wæs god cyning!* (11), "That was a good king!" (line 11). Later in the poem, when Hildeburg stands looking over the battlefield where her son and her brother have died fighting on opposite sides, *þæt wæs geomuru ides!* (1075), "That was a sad woman!" And later yet, Grendel's pool evokes the formula in negative terms: *Nis þæt heoru stow!* "That is not a happy place!" (1372).

Knowing that my audience will not recognize standard formulas as the poet's audience did, I have not been faithful to this feature, often omitting, for example, "that was" in the formula described above. I have, however, tried to preserve such direct repetitions as "in those long ago days of this fleeting life" (lines 790 and 806). The two translations I have immediately at hand, good ones, ignore this repetition.

I have been sparing with compounds. This practice distinguishes my translation most vividly from the "Anglo-Saxon" verse of Pound and his followers, and it was a reluctant choice, because compounding is an important element in Anglo-Saxon poetic diction. But I felt that the grittiness and density of such diction interfered with my primary aim: to achieve clarity in a resonant narrative verse that moves as freely as prose. Perhaps I shall come to regret, as Nabokov regrets about his first translation of *The Song of Igor's Campaign*, making the poem "much too readable." If so, my major regret will be the simplification of compounds. But now, I think it will be a boon to the reader.

As a further boon I have deleted certain of those characters whom Klaeber lists in his glossary of names, when they appear simply as patronymics; I have also, at many points, named a character where the poet uses merely a pronoun. I have simplified the spelling of certain names to make them more easily pronounced in Modern English.

Following Marianne Moore's "ban on dead words," I have avoided diction which has been deadened, especially by Victorian translators' attempts to medievalize a text, but I have on the other hand included a series of Old English words which have a technical meaning and give a flavor to the poem that I like: *byrnie, atheling, shope, thane, wyrd, sark, mere* and *thule*. These, too, I have spelled so that they will be given the proper pronunciation, or some equivalent of it, by a modern reader untrained in Old English orthography. I am fond of these words, and justify their inclusion against Miss Moore's ban by the fact that they are not archaic so much as actively foreign, words transferred over from the language (and the society) of their origin. I translate these words in footnotes on their first appearance.

I have concentrated on reproducing the sound structure of the language in the alliterative verse form, in the names, and in the few untranslated words listed above. So far as I am aware, in only the first word of the poem, *what* for *hwæt*, have I allowed the sound actually to dictate meaning. There the liberty seemed justified. Other than the *what* exception, I have tried to reproduce, within the strictures of the meter, the meaning of the words as I understand them, either literally or approximately. When my understanding of the meaning varies significantly from Klaeber's (upon whose text my translation is based), I discuss the discrepancy in a note.

There are passages of heightened rhetoric in the original. These are marked most overtly by the transverse alliteration mentioned earlier, by variation (a sequence of phrases saying nearly the same thing in different ways), and by expanded meter (longer lines). I try to capture the feeling of such passages through diction. But I consider it a mistake to heighten the diction when the poet does not foreground a passage himself—a mistake, but a temptation, especially when the passage offers undeveloped material. The question here, and it is one that all literary translators must face, is how far is one at liberty to "improve" the text, if one feels in tune with it? Even a conscientious balancing, introducing more "quality" into one passage because it was lost in another, may shift the poet's emphasis, though to some degree such balancing is inevitable. All literary translations come of a partnership in which the junior partner will leave his or her mark, showing greater or less dedication to preserve the original depending on how much desire there is to make it a personal document. Among recent translators of *Beowulf*, one introduces a meter marked by a frequent caesura after the first word of the line, another, a fine one, tries to compensate for the puns lost in translation by introducing his own, a third emends the text (following suggestions by certain scholars) without warning the reader that he is doing so. Believing that my readers would like to think that they are enjoying the same poem that might have been chanted in an Anglo-Saxon hall, I have tried to avoid such temptations to "improve" on the original, either by introducing personal stylistic elements as those translators above have done, or even by developing suggestions dropped, intentionally or not, by the poet himself. (I should acknowledge here my debt to previous translators; even those I am criticizing have done much to influence my own choices, and that influence marks another form of junior partnership. As John Ciardi said of his predecessors in translating Dante, "Without their failures I should never have attempted my own.")

For the Anglo-Saxons, honor, luck and fate were related concepts having connotations different from what they have for us today. I have not translated the words for these ideas consistently, even though they are key words in the moral structure of the narrative. I have felt it best at each occurrence to give such concepts the nuance that will convey to a modern audience the meaning that they have in Old English, or that I believe they have, within each particular context in this poem. For example, Beowulf would identify himself with the role of the Germanic warrior-hero (see lines 1386–87); it is by praiseworthy deeds, by first making a commitment then carrying it out, that such an identity is first established and then maintained. Beowulf is the most courteous of warriors, but that courtesy does not include the concept of modesty, as it would for a Christian knight of the later middle ages. Saying what one hopes to be capable of and then carrying out those words in deeds is the proper behavior of a warrior. This is demonstrated by the whole interchange between Unferth, Beowulf, Wealtheow and Hrothgar in lines 499–661. After the verbal match with Unferth which reveals Beowulf's previous experience as a monster-slayer, Beowulf says he will "behave with fitting courage" when Grendel comes that night, even if he dies in the attempt. Wealtheow the queen "liked well those noble words/ of the Geat's pledge." Later we are reminded of that pledge when Beowulf "remembered his evening speech, stood up, /gripped fast against (Grendel)" (759–60). Because the nuance of the significant word here, *beot*, is so different from "boast," as it is often translated, I have given it particular attention, translating it almost uniformly as "pledge," which is what it more properly means. "Pledge" avoids the negative connotations of "boast," connotations inappropriate to the noble act Beowulf is pre-performing in words.

Related to this problem of terms associated with honor is the last word in the poem, *lofgeornost*, which may be translated literally "most eager for glory." This is probably the most discussed word in Old English poetry. The discussion is analogous to that of Plato's *aretê*, in that the usual translation of this Greek word, "virtue," carries a moral nuance lacking in the original, which more properly means "excellence." It seems to me that saying Beowulf was "most eager for glory" comes as near to the heroic feeling of the original as describing his and Wiglaf's slaying of the dragon as an act of "pluck." Again Christian modesty has intervened to create a moral ambivalence perhaps not present in the original—certainly not present to those who use the word in the world of the poem, where *lof* is a quality to be sought by warriors. In view of this heroic context, I have translated the last word of the poem "most earnest for esteem." As well as retaining the social basis of Beowulf's desire ("glory" is egocentric whereas "esteem" implies the positive judgment of others), this translation preserves the dignity implied in *lofgeornost*, the final word of praise by the Geatish people for their beloved, grave and noble warrior king.

The Italics

My primary purpose for using italics is aesthetic, for clarity and style. Many people reading *Beowulf* for the first time find it difficult to organize the story in their minds, simply because it is unlike anything else they have ever read. *Beowulf* is a highly digressive poem; the fairy tale exploits of the hero appear side-by-side with factual history, mythic history, moral comment and scriptural allusion so that at one moment the reader may be engrossed in the main story and at the next moment floundering in a digression, sometimes without any apparent change of subject or even of pronoun reference for guidance. I have italicized these digressions, and while the italics represent visually on the page one of the poem's outstanding characteristics, at the same time they alert and orient the reader as the poet moves from narrative into commentary.

The italics also highlight and distinguish a major theme of the poem which I believe reveals the Anglo-Saxon poet's purpose in composing a story about a Scandinavian culture hero, a hero of another time and place. I have said above that *Beowulf* is a social poem; I believe that the poet's purpose was political, to realign the antecedents of his society in a way more acceptable to his contemporaries. I have on the whole italicized only the lengthier asides which put the action within this larger perspective.

In the first part of the poem, set in Denmark, the italicized passages consist chiefly of scriptural allusions not accessible to the pagan protagonists, to whom scripture has not yet been revealed, or of moral commentary or reflection intended as an aside to his audience by the poet. In the second part of the poem, set in the land of the Geats, the italicized passages are mostly episodes and digressions having more to do with Scandinavian history than with Beowulf's exploits as a hero. In the case of the Finnsburg episode (a historical digression), I have continued the italics to include Wealtheow's apparent response to the story, a response which may be interpreted as predictive of historical events to follow. Another long italicized passage, 2032–2143, contains Beowulf's assessment of the Danish court, again predictive, followed by an account of his exploits in Denmark, essentially a summing up of his previous two monster fights. Every passage in italics contains some material relevant to cosmic, Scandinavian or moral history. The reader intent only on the heroic story may skim over these asides, which are invaluable for the wider view they afford but are not precisely part of the narrative.

That they may be skimmed over does not mean that these passages should be undervalued. Much of the grandeur of Beowulf in the Danish part of the poem is the result of his heroic role in a monster feud having cosmic origins which he cannot perceive. Much of the tragedy in the Geatish part of the poem is the result of his and his people's sacrifice when surrounded by historical forces of destruction even more potent than demon or dragon. Those passages that add the further dimensions of scriptural and Scandinavian history are there if you want to see them, but they are not the main story. They function rather like a harmonic development in music, not part of the main tune but capable of turning a folksong into a symphony.

Here is a list of the passages I have italicized and their most important subject matter:

Lines	Subject (with available dates)
105–114	Cain's exile and progeny.
178–188	Comment on the heathen Danes.
898–915	Sigemund and Beowulf contrasted with Heremod.
1063–1191	The Finnsburg story and Wealtheow's response to it.
1197–1215	The story of Hama, and the fall of Hygelac in Frisia (ca. 521).
1261–1276	Grendel's descent from Cain.
1688–1699	The engraving of the Flood and the runes of the giant swordhilt.
1931–1962	The story of Offa and Thryth.
2032–2143	Beowulf's report to his king on politics in Heorot and his slaying of the two monsters.

As may be seen from the contents, these passages are not those isolated by Adrien Bonjour in *The Digressions in Beowulf*, passages which contain much of immediate interest for the plot (such as the burial of the dragon's treasure). Rather these extend and authenticate the world of the story for the poet's audience and for us. They set the exploits of the Geatish hero within a framework that first recognizes the nobility of ancestral pagans by aligning them with the "right" side in the cosmic feud between good and evil, and later salvages their historical obscurity by offering an epic conclusion to their tribal existence on the continent. I like to think that the Anglo-Saxon poet celebrated Beowulf as a Scandinavian culture hero sanctioning the poet's own ancestral past.

Having designed this text for oral as well as for silent reading, I begin and end the italics at points convenient for continuity. When a break occurs at the half-line, I have usually maintained alliteration before and after the italicized passage so that the reading need not falter.

My hope is that this version of Beowulf reads as easily as a prose narrative but with some of the compulsive power of a poem, whether it is being read silently or aloud, as a whole or abridged. My hope is that it is so transparent that one may pass through it into the world the poet envisioned, of an age before his own.

The Pictures

The pictures accompanying the text add a dimension of quite a different kind, making the world of the poem real by translating verbal descriptions into visual images. Only with recent archaeological discoveries has it become clear how accurately the *Beowulf* poet is describing the objects of worth in his poem; the monsters may be highly symbolic aggressors, but the poet's reconstruction of the material culture of the society upon which they prey accords largely with the facts. For example, a few decades ago in England a great treasure was discovered in a mound at Sutton Hoo in East Anglia, containing among other objects some fine Swedish armor and a sixth century masked helmet that corresponds in detail to helmets described in *Beowulf*. Just recently another, later, such helmet has been discovered in York; it is reproduced on the dust jacket of this book. I have concluded the picture series with a Swedish memorial stone upon which the final lines of *Beowulf* are echoed in a runic inscription.

Place and Date
of the Artifacts

The many pictures of artifacts and manuscript drawings throughout the text show how other artists, roughly contemporary with the Anglo-Saxon poet or with the earlier period of his story, have depicted many of the same objects or features that he mentions, from helmets with boars' heads above the cheekplates to the dragon biting around his victim's neck. These artifacts from outside the story, designed by artists who knew nothing of *Beowulf*, give the poem a credibility within a material dimension that has not been available before.

As much as possible the illustrations for this translation have been chosen from artifacts and manuscripts contemporary with the poem or its events. Those few which come from a later date are based on traditional themes.

Jacket front panel: Anglo-Saxon helmet discovered at Coppergate in York on 12 May 1982. England, probably late seventh or early eighth century.

Frontispiece: Mask helmet found in the ship cenotaph at Sutton Hoo, England. Ca. 600 A.D.

p. vi   Centerpiece, Book of Durrow, folio 192^v. Ireland, ca. 680 A.D.

Facing p. 1: Initial (inverted) from the Lindisfarne Gospels, folio 90^r. England, ca. 700 A.D. Spear Warrior: Design from a picture stone found at Skokloster, Uppland. Sweden, ca. 700 A.D.

p. 2   Twisted Prow: Detail of the reconstruction of the ship found at Oseberg, Norway. Ca. 800 A.D.

p. 4   Harp-Lyre: Reconstruction of an instrument excavated at Sutton Hoo, England. Ca. 600 A.D.

p. 5   Satan in the Mouth of Hell: Detail from Bodleian Library MS. Junius ll; 10, 3. England, tenth or eleventh century. The mouth of Hell is often a dragon's jaws. In Celtic and Scandinavian tradition alike, the head of the dragon frequently resembles that of a lion, perhaps following Byzantine models and deriving ultimately from the Far East; the reptilian dragon head is of a later period.

pp. 6–7   Head: Wooden carving on a sleigh found in the ship burial at Oseberg, Norway. Ca. 800 A.D.

pp. 8–9   Ship with Twisted Prow: Detail from a picture stone found at Tjängvide, Götland, Sweden. Ca. 700 A.D.

p. 10   Coppergate Helmet: Anglo-Saxon, probably late seventh or early eighth century (see cover).

p. 11   Boar's Head over Cheekplate (drawing): Detail from the Coppergate Helmet (see above and cover). The same detail occurs on the masked

Acknowledgement is made to the following persons and museums for photographs of artifacts in their collections and the permission to publish these copyright items:

Denmark
To the National Museum, Copenhagen, for photographs on pages 44, 55, 83, 85.

France
To the Musée des Antiquités Nationales, St. Germain–en–Laye, for the photograph on page 96.

Ireland
To Trinity College, Dublin, for photographs on pages vi, 12–13, 18–19, 70, 81, 86–87, 93, 114–115.

Netherlands
To the Bibliotheek der Rijksuniversitet, Utrecht, for the photograph on page 64.

Norway
To Ernst Schwitters, photographer, in Lysaket, for his fine photograph of "Grendel" on pages 6–7.
To the University Museum of National Antiquities, Oslo, for the photographs on pages 2, 21, 22, 42, 57, 80–81, 88–89, 92–93, 107, 110.

Sweden
To Götlands Fornsal, Visby, Götland, for photographs on pages 8–9, 23, 34, 40–41, 52–53, 68–69, 74, 113.

To the Statens Historiska Museum, Stockholm, for the photographs and sources of drawings on pages 1, 14, 15, 25, 30, 36–37, 39, 43, 44, 46, 49, 50–51, 72–73, 76–77, 77, 78, 82, 86, 91, 94, 108–109, 112, 113, 123.

United Kingdom
To P.V. Addyman, M.A., F.S.A., for his assistance in obtaining pictures of the newly discovered Coppergate Helmet (pages 10 and 11), and to M.S. Duffy, photographer for the York Archaeological Trust, for the cover photograph of the Coppergate Helmet.
To the Bodleian Library, Oxford, for the manuscript drawing on page 5.
To the British Library, London, for the manuscript illumination and drawing on pages 1 and 47.
To the British Museum, London, for the photographs of the frontispiece and on pages 4, 17, 26, 28–29, 31, 35, 38, 48, 58–59, 60, 63, 66–67, 71, 97, 100–101, 103, 104–105, 106, 111.
To the National Museum of Antiquities of Scotland, Edinburgh, for the photograph on page 95.

United States
To Karen Reynolds Glosecki for the block print on pages 72–73.
To the Walters Art Gallery, Baltimore, Maryland, for the photograph on page 99.

Notes to the Translation

These notes mainly concern customs and interpretations of the action. The language of the text itself is discussed only when there is a dispute about meaning, or when the translation offers an unorthodox interpretation of a passage and I feel I must defend it, or when the expression is so fine in the original that I feel compelled to call critical attention to it.

Like the translation, the notes are based for the most part on Klaeber's edition, from which I often quote. The other scholar most often cited is C. L. Wrenn, also an editor of the poem and my tutor at Oxford. The influence of R. W. Chambers' monumental *Beowulf: An Introduction* (London: Cambridge University Press, third edition, 1959) may be found throughout these pages, as can that of my first teacher of *Beowulf*, Fred C. Robinson.

Three Anglo-Saxon letters are used in these notes in Old English words: æ("ash"), ð("eth") and þ("thorn"). The first is a vowel sound with the value of the *a* in ash, the others are *th* sounds.

1 *Hwæt* is a standard formulaic opening for a heroic poem in Old English, often translated "lo!" or "listen!" It has been suggested that *hwæt* may have been accompanied by a loud thrum on the round-harp, or more technically the "harp-lyre," that is often mentioned in association with poetry recited in the hall.

4 Shield (Old English *Scyld*) is known in Scandinavian legend as Skjoldr and is described by Saxo Grammaticus as a great king and warrior, but the accounts of his waif-like arrival and his magnificent ship-burial at sea are thought by some scholars to be derived from English legends about Sheaf (Shield's father). Sheaf's wonderful arrival appears in the chronicles of Ethelward and William of Malmesbury, and until quite recently there existed in England a custom of floating a sheaf of wheat down a river on a shield to ensure the fertility of the fields. The Danes, however, were called the sons of Shield (Scyldingas), which probably originated from a descriptive nickname, like Spear-Danes, and in turn gave rise to a myth about a racial ancestor, "Shield." (An ancestor who is created on the basis of a name already in use, to explain it, is called "eponymous.") The poet himself may have shifted the arrival story from Sheaf to Shield in order to retain the myth and the evocative ship-burial, the ritual of which is echoed at the end of the poem, and to connect this myth with the "ancestor" of the Danes whose strong rule made possible the kingdom which Heorot later dominates. The Shield prelude also sets the tone for the whole poem. Klaeber compares Shield's destiny to that of Tennyson's King Arthur; "from the great deep to the great deep he goes." A closer and more relevant analogy is the swallow parable of King Edwin's hall-councillor: "He quickly flies through the hall, comes in through one door and through the other door out again he goes, from winter into winter again . . . thus is this life of man: what went before or what follows after we do not know" (Bede, *History*, II, 13).

5 "taking their mead-seats": As often is his practice, the poet refers here to the whole (the hall) by the part (the mead-seats), in much the same way as someone might refer to his "country seat" or "ancestral seat" today, meaning a big country house that has been in the family for a long time. The mead-bench, probably rather resembling a church pew, was a highly important ritual object in early Germanic society, as the dispensing of mead was one of those ceremonies which bound society together. To "deprive a tribe of its mead-seats" was to destroy its spirit.

36 "by the mast": Shield was probably placed in a seated position with his back against the mast, like the dead warriors in the Vendel ship-graves excavated in this century. The findings of burial goods at Sutton Hoo in 1939 show that the descriptions of treasures in the burials of Shield and Beowulf need not be ascribed to "poetic extravagance" as they formerly were. This early Anglo-Saxon treasure, containing items from places as remote as Sweden and Byzantium, has been described as "the most valuable treasure ever found on English soil."

49 One authority states categorically, "We know from Scandinavian graves . . . that the illustrious dead were buried . . . in ships, with their bows to sea-ward; that they were, however, not sent to sea, but were either burnt in that position or mounded over with earth." It is of course difficult to prove that there was or was not actual sea-burial, since any remains would be lost to archaeology; in Norse literature the ships were sometimes set on fire as well as being "given to the sea." Both Shield's coming and his going, however, appear to be highly metaphorical.

53 The narrative of Beowulf's adventures begins here, with the first numbered fit. The first fifty-two lines have been called an "exordium" and a "prelude."

69–70 For the translation "a mighty hall . . . that the sons of men should hear of forever" see Fred C. Robinson's textual study of these lines in *TSL*, 11 (1966), 151–160.

78 Heorot: In the Norse analogues the Danish court is named Hleithr (Latin Lethra, probably modern Leire), which alliterates, as does Heorot, with the names of the royal family, Hrothgar, Hrothulf, etc. The Anglo-Saxon name of the hall in *Beowulf* and in *Widsith* (line 49) was probably symbolic of royalty; a hart cult in both Celtic and Germanic tradition is well attested by archaeological finds as well as literary references. (Sigurd, for example, is surrounded by hart symbolism.)

82–85 The poet continually foreshadows events to come, some of which do not even take place in the poem, like the burning of Heorot. "The sword-hatred of a son-in-law" is clarified by Beowulf himself in lines 2024–69 (see note).

88 It is the nature of such "exiled demons" to be angered by the sounds of good fellowship in the hall, but the *Beowulf* poet gives this theme a peculiarly Christian twist. Through the *shope's* song of creation, the hall, where the inhabitants lived happily "until One from Hell began to perform evil deeds," is identified with Eden by means of a scriptural passage addressed by the poet exclusively to us, his Christian audience.

106 The idea of the descent of monsters and evil spirits or giants from Cain and of the destruction of the giants by the Flood (see lines 1688–93) is ultimately derived from the scriptural narrative by a continuous reading of the Cain story (Genesis 4) through the account of giants (Genesis 6:2–4), Jehovah's disgust (6:5–7), and the story of Noah (Genesis 7). According to Irish belief, Cham, the son of Noah, inherited the curse of Cain and became the progenitor of monsters. In the *Beowulf* manuscript, *caines* (line 107) is altered from original *cames* (Cham?), which has suggested to some scholars a Celtic background for the *Beowulf* poet.

112 *orcs,* Old English *orc-neas,* refers to the walking dead.

156–158 "to settle with gold . . . compensation" is legal terminology; Grendel's relationship to the Danes is here presented as a feud, under the rules of which a slaying may be paid for in *wergild* (I accept the OED explanation "man gold" rather than "covenant gold"), whereby peaceful relationships may theoretically be renewed. The "bright compensation" (158) is gold, and the contrast between the brightness of the gold as a sign of renewed friendship and the darkness of Grendel (159) is, of course, symbolic.

168–169 A more literal translation, highlighting the problems, might be as follows: "He could not approach that gift-throne, the treasure in front of the lord (the Treasure, i.e. altar?, because of the Lord?), nor know his (the lord's/the Lord's) love."

This is one of the great cruces in the poem, not because any particular word is difficult, but because editors and commentators have disagreed about what the words refer to. Most editors have attempted to unravel it (literally) either by making the *gifstol* (gift-throne) the throne in Heorot and making the lord Hrothgar, or by changing the location of the lines to come between 110 and 111, so that *he* can refer to Cain and the throne and lord both take on Christian connotations.

Since Latin writers of the period take full advantage of the figure called *serta,* where classical allusion is interwoven with the contemporary subject, I suspect that the skilled and literate *Beowulf* poet is doing something similar here, interweaving Christianity with his subject in such a way that Grendel is identified with Cain (as elsewhere in the poem) and the throne of Hrothgar with the throne of God, while yet keeping the main focus on the action in Heorot. The fact that "mankind's foe . . . that fiend in exile" is the logical antecedent of the pronoun *he* very much enhances the double focus.

While *myne* (168) can mean "love," it might better be translated "remembrance" or even "communion"—keeping both the Christian and secular implications, since the Old Norse *minni* drink was a memorial toast to dead kinsmen to aid them in the other world. The point being made here is that Grendel, "the terrible one who goes alone," has no communion (the most vital thing in life for Christians and pagans alike) with anybody.

175–188 The idol worship of the Danes and the poet's Christian exhortations mark the most vivid contrast in the poem between pagan (or in this case heathen) and Christian belief. The Christian poet offers only two alternatives for the afterlife, the embrace of fire or of the Father (183–188); he has himself set up the debate, so actively engaged in by some scholars while scorned by others, concerning the destiny of Beowulf's soul.

204 *hæl,* which I have translated "lots," is found in Wülker's *Glossaries* in various forms, meaning "augury," "omen," "divination." For an imaginative reconstruction of the way runes might have been used as lots, and a series of practice "games" of increasing complexity for the modern reader, see my and Stella Longland's *Rune Games* (Routledge, 1982).

259 *wordhord unleac* "unlocked his hoard of word-treasure" is a formulaic opening for a formal speech, found in *Widsith, Andreas,* and other Old English poems.

308 Gold-ornamented halls abound in folk tales and in the Norse sagas. Adam of Bremen gives a second-hand description of the great pagan temple at Uppsala with its serrated ornament which looked to his informers like a golden chain hanging above the roof between the gables. This is only one of several pieces of evidence suggesting that roofs of important halls really did sometimes gleam with gold, and that perhaps we should not ascribe the poet's description of Heorot entirely to poetic fancy, as scholars did the extravagant ship-burials before the discovery of the Sutton Hoo treasure. Germanic and Celtic chiefs had immense gold hoards, and much of the ritual of the society was based on display; one felt safe with one's fellows glittering with golden armor in a high and gold-adorned hall.

320 The road to Heorot was formerly thought to be imagined by the poet as paved after the Roman fashion, but the archaeologist Rosemary Cramp has pointed out that stone roads leading to important Germanic halls have been found in countries where the Romans did not penetrate. In 1815 the earliest critic of *Beowulf,* a Dane named Grundtvig, picked out this detail as proof that the poem was composed in England where Romans had built *stanfah* ("stone paved") roads; from this he argued that *Beowulf* was therefore not a translation from a Scandinavian original, as the earliest editor had supposed. But the integral Christian element in the poem, which was composed before Christianity was a familiar faith in the Scandinavian north, gives us all the proof we need that *Beowulf* is an English poem.

325 (and 397) It was the rule at all periods to deposit weapons outside before entering a hall. In provincial Swedish almost every church porch is called *våpenhus* "weapon house," because the worshippers used to leave their arms there before they entered.

359 "Before the shoulders" is a standard term meaning "in front," but with the implication of a relatively lower status. Hildeburh's son is placed in this relationship to Hnaef on the funeral pyre at Finnsburh, *eame on eaxle* "at his uncle's shoulder" (1117), but the dead fire-dragon lies *on efn* "just beside" (2903) and *wiðerræhtes* "opposite" (3039) in relation to Beowulf, with no intimation of lesser importance.

408–409 Such an immediate identification of kinship and valor is typical of self-introduction both in epic poetry and in the diplomatic interchanges of actual tribal society. It would stand as an insult to Hrothgar's nobility to be approached by a stranger not able to establish an honorable position in the hierarchy of noble men.

433–441 Beowulf's chivalry "makes a modern impression," says Klaeber. Beowulf decides to fight the monster on the latter's own primitive terms, hand to hand, not knowing beforehand that Grendel cannot be harmed by ordinary weapons.

446 Most editors explain this "hiding of the head" as the custom of covering the dead man's head with a cloth. The sense of the passage is simply that nothing will remain of Beowulf if cannibalistic Grendel has his way. I suspect that the "hiding of the head" involves a custom rather more grim than that postulated by Klaeber and others: why is it necessary for Wiglaf to hold "guard over the heads" of Beowulf and the dragon later (2910), and why does the use made of Ashere's head (1420–22) have such ritual impact? Anne Ross, in *Pagan Celtic Britain,* offers interesting speculations and archaeological evidence concerning prehistoric head cults in Britain.

454 Wayland: Klaeber says, "If a weapon or armor in Old Germanic literature was attributed to Wayland, this was conclusive proof of its superior workmanship and venerable associations. The figure of this wondrous smith—the Germanic Vulcanus (Hephaistos)—symbolizing at first the marvels of metal working as they impressed the people of the stone age, was made the subject of a heroic legend which spread from North Germany to Scandinavia and England." The myth of Wayland persisted into recent times: there is a Wayland the Smith's Cave in Berkshire, and Sir Walter Scott refers to Wayland in *Kenilworth.*

459–472 Beowulf's father had been involved in a feud after which the Geats compelled him to leave their country for fear of reprisals. He sought out Hrothgar, who paid compensation (wergild) to the Wylfings on his behalf; in return Edgetheow "swore oaths" of peace or allegiance to Hrothgar. (The only difficulty with this simple explanation is that it is based on an editorial emendation of the text, *gara cyn to wedera cyn,* i.e., the Geats. Kemp Malone suggests that Edgetheow was a Wylfing in origin who received a judicial sentence of banishment for a term, in *Studies in Heroic Legend and Current Speech,* pp. 108–115.)

466 "Jewelled kingdom" is a return to the manuscript text, *gimme rice,* for which Fred C. Robinson argues in *Speculum,* 52 (1977), p. 191.

501 "unbound his battle-runes" is a phrase describing manner of speech rather than an interesting pagan custom concerning rune-staves; but as Unferth is a *thule*, a word that has associations with oratory, the phrase may have technical implications. Recently, Carol Clover, in a paper on "Ritual Insult in Germanic Tradition," related Unferth's taunt directly to the Scandinavian traditional word-battle described in the sagas. Unferth's name, which Klaeber interprets as *unfrith*, "mar-peace," suggests also that it is his official function to taunt such newcomers as Beowulf. The effect of his taunt is to provoke Beowulf to recount his boyhood feat in such a way as to give him added credibility as a monster-killer.

570 "God's beacon," the sun, enables Beowulf to see the shore after the storm. Notice other descriptions of dawn and the references to the sun and to the breaking forth of light throughout the poem.

572–573 This is almost proverbial. "Fortune favors the brave," but it by no means renders manly courage unnecessary. Wrenn points out that "the same idea is almost exactly repeated in 2291–3," but with God mentioned instead of *wyrd*.

587–589 Believing that *þinum broðrum* is what Klaeber calls a "generic plural" like *bearnum ond broðrum* at line 1074, I have translated this as a singular. Unferth has murdered his kinsman, probably the worst crime possible in a tribal society, yet he remains a prominent and respected statesman. Though there are analogues for this, it is very odd. Beowulf tells Unferth that he will receive his due reward in Hell, even though his mental powers are great, in "the most specifically Christian language so far found in the poem" (Wrenn). Is Unferth a "civilized" member of the *clanna* Cain? It should be noted that Beowulf appears to have an innate understanding of good and evil, divine judgment and punishment; this is called "natural knowledge" by theologians, and is described by Paul in his letter to the Romans as a type of religious understanding available to all men, including noble pagans. The poet is, however, very careful to keep comments about scriptural history, which could only be known to those in the the poem through a teacher, separate from their understanding. Beowulf can know about judgment and damnation, but not about Cain.

620 "The Helming lady" must be a member of that Wylfing tribe among which Beowulf's father slew Heatholaf (lines 460–461), as Helm is called a ruler of the Wylfings in *Widsith*, line 29. Some have suggested that the Wuffingas of East Anglia (and of the great Sutton Hoo treasure) are descendants of the Wylfings mentioned in *Beowulf*; others argue against this interesting but speculative identification.

622–624 The royal lady is here directing that Germanic drinking ceremony which seals heterogeneous members of the tribe and its followers into a dedicated group. Her approach to Beowulf is a separate ritual as she offers him the cup, not in his turn where he sits among the others, but after it has gone the round.

660–661 Hrothgar's promise of a reward is what is expected of a good king (compare 20–25); it does not detract, in the modern sense of payment or bribery, from the nobility of the hero, but rather does both him and his "gold friend" honor.

697 *wigspeda gewiofu* "weaving of luck in battle" is usually taken as a mere figure of speech, like *hel* in line 852. But in *Njal's Saga*, Chapter 157, a man called Dorrud looked through a window-slit in a woman's house, "and there he saw women with a loom set up before them. Men's heads were used in place of weights, and human entrails in place of the warp and woof: a sword served as the treadle and an arrow as the batten." As the women wove they spoke verses that would "weave war-luck" in the battle of Clontarf.

703 The sleep of the Geats in this situation has aroused much speculation; it has been suggested that both this sleep and the fact that Beowulf waits on his bed while one of his retainers is being devoured are features of the original story which the poet has not successfully adapted.

710–722 Klaeber, comparing the Grendel fight to a more straightforward monster fight in Old Norse prose, objects to the interrupted narrative presented here by the poet. Many modern critics find it among the most satisfyingly artistic passages of the poem. Renoir, speaking of it in cinematic terms, visualizes Grendel's approach as long shot, medium shot, close-up, extreme close-up: "He came in the dark night . . . he came from the moor . . . he came to the building . . . a horrible light poured out of his eyes . . . " The stylistic device of variation, in which the same thing is said in more than one way, is used by the poet to build up dramatic tension and meaning simultaneously.

725 *fagne flor* "decorated floor" or "colored floor": Most recent commentators on this line refer to the place name Fawler, shown by charters to have been derived from Old English *fag flor*, and they mention the well-attested fact that Roman mosaic floors have been found near at least two villages of this name. This has suggested that the "colored floor" in Heorot may have been conceived by the poet as a mosaic floor. Elsewhere in the poem, however, a wooden floor is suggested. This by no means cancels out the possibility of a highly ornamented floor, perhaps with a painted design at least in part based, like certain "carpet pages" of such manuscripts as the Book of Kells and the Lindisfarne Gospels, on Roman pavements.

726–727 Several demonic characteristics are shared by the monster Grendel and the Green Knight of the Middle English *Sir Gawain and the Green Knight*. Both seem to be drawn by harmonious music to the hall; both seem to cast those in the hall into a magical trance (*as al were slypped vpon slepe*, SGGK, line 244; the *Gawain* poet perhaps incorporates this traditional element better than the *Beowulf* poet does); both glance around the hall with a demonic light in their eyes (*Beowulf* 727, SGGK 119–202). The structures of these two stories also bear many similarities.

727 "light like a flame": Fire imagery is connected with demonic beings throughout *Beowulf*.

740–782 These lines, on folio 148 of the manuscript, were found between lines 91 and 92 (folios 133 and 134) by those who first recorded their examination of the poem in modern times. Presumably the person who bound *Beowulf* together with Augustine's *Soliloquies* into the codex now known as "The Nowell Codex" accidentally misplaced this folio in his binding. In part because of this displacement, for a century the poem was thought to be about "Beowulf, a certain Dane who waged wars against the kings of Sweden" (Langebec). It is an interesting exercise to read the text this way (remembering that I have clarified many pronouns which were loosely or not at all identified by the poet) in order to sample the kind of difficulties that were faced by the earliest modern readers of the poem.

740–745 The description of Grendel devouring Handscio passes so quickly in a heightened oral reading that I think it explains why Beowulf did not intervene to save his friend's life: he did not have time!

748–749 There are differences of opinion about the form of this first hold in the great wrestling match. Does Beowulf rise to a sitting position, supported by his arm, or does he reach out to grasp Grendel's arm? The effect achieved by Crossley-Holland in his translation seems to me to parallel that intended by the poet: Beowulf immediately grasped Grendel's evil intentions and set himself against that arm. He doesn't stand up until 759. (Chambers, in the note on these lines in his edition, offers a different account.)

765–769 The combat in Heorot is described partly in ironic terms as a "dinner party" for Grendel: He enters the hall with delighted anticipation of a meal (730–734), enjoys his main course (Handscio, 740–745), Beowulf remembers his after dinner speech (758–759), "ale" is shared out (767–769), and finally Grendel sings a "lay" (782–788). E. B. Irving, Jr., discusses this ironic substructure in *A Reading of Beowulf* (London, 1968). The general intention of this passage would seem to be (as Irving has suggested) that the noise in the hall is much like that of a wild drinking session, but without the kind of fellowship usually involved (see the note on *myne*, 169). The irony is extended even further by the references to Heorot's "mouth" through which Grendel enters (723–725) and to the flames which will in turn "swallow" the hall (781–782).

836 Scholars are still undecided whether the arm has been hung inside or outside the hall: the general opinion is that it is outside. Eilert Ekwall says, "The placing of Grendel's arm above the entrance reminds me of a custom prevalent in the countryside of Sweden at least till about fifty years ago, *viz*, to nail a dead hawk or kite or other bird of prey over the door of the stable or perhaps some other house, doubtless for protection or luck. Grendel's arm may have been placed over the door of Heorot not only as a trophy."

874 *wordum wrixlan* "to mingle his words": Wrenn suggests that this is an allusion to the practice of variation, the repetition of similar ideas in different words so typical of Anglo-Saxon poetry. Others have argued that it refers to the Germanic method of composition by oral

formulas, or that it means "to weave words" rather as serpentine ornaments are "woven" or interlaced in Anglo-Saxon art. Yet another group of critics believes that the phrase refers to *paronomasia*, or word-play. Word-play does occur in this passage. It was noticed years ago that through lines 867–871 there are echoes of *secg* and *munde*, and it may be that here the *Beowulf* poet is offering us an example of the very practice that he claims for Hrothgar's *shope*. I favor this argument, but no one knows exactly what *wordum wrixlan* refers to.

874–900 Klaeber points out that the Sigemund story given here is an epitome combining two separate stories, one about the hero's adventures with his nephew Fitela, and another about his dragon fight. Wrenn says, "Here, more clearly than in some of the other episodes and digressions, we see the deliberate and most effective art of the poet." The parallel with Beowulf's later fight with the dragon, and the contrast in that he loses his life in that fight, would be apparent immediately to an audience familiar with these stories.

885 *dom* "glory" after his death was the Germanic hero's chief aim in life, the purpose of his great deeds.

887 In *Cotton maxims II* we are told, *Draca sceal on hlæwe, frod, frætwum wlanc* "the dragon will bide in the barrow, wise, proud of his treasures." This theme, as well as that of the heat of devilish beings, is picked up again in the second half of the poem.

901–915 Klaeber comments at length upon the Heremod digression and its Danish historical and legendary analogues, which show Heremod to have been a traditional figure in the legendary history of Denmark; even the connection with Sigemund is traditional. But, while the earlier scholar Müllenhoff's interpretation of Heremod as simply an allegorical personification of *here-mod* "warlike disposition" is thus proved invalid, the king does have this allegorical function in *Beowulf*, through aptness of name rather than allegory *per se*. (Another digression on Heremod comes in Hrothgar's long speech, at lines 1709–22.) The chief purpose of the Heremod digression is, as the poet makes clear in lines 913–915, to describe Beowulf in terms of what he is not: he is not like Heremod. A basic message of the first part of the poem is contained in the stories of these two famous men: Be like Sigemund, who won esteem by active valor, killing the dragon, not like Heremod, who was so oppressed by his own misery that he murdered his friends.

916–917 The Sigemund-Heremod digression is bracketed between references to horse racing. This device, used often by the poet, is called an "envelope pattern." The whole poem is contained within the envelope pattern of heroic funerals.

947 It was a standard practice and one way of ensuring loyalty and friendship to adopt a child from another powerful tribe or family. (See the note below on lines 2428–29.)

978 *dom* "judgment": This is the first direct reference to a *dom* different from that esteem or glory won by secular deeds (see the note on 885). For pagan Beowulf's "natural knowledge" of the Creator and his ways, see the note on lines 587–588.

994–996 Long picture tapestries, six to nine inches wide, were found in the Oseberg ship-burial. The Bayeux tapestry is about one and a half feet wide by 132 feet long. These so-called tapestries, really embroidered picture strips, were traditionally hung along a hall to decorate it for a banquet, much as we use banners and bunting today in our much rarer hall ceremonies.

1007–08 The theme of sleep after the banquet is here being used metaphorically: all men sleep in death after the banquet of life. (On another level, however, it concludes the ironic sub-theme of Grendel's "party" at Heorot.)

1053–54 Hrothgar compensates the Geats for their loss of a man by paying them *wergild* "man gold." This is a standard legal practice, but one which also does the dead man honor. (See the note on lines 156–158.)

1065–70 Hrothgar's *shope* is singing about how disaster came upon Finn's son(s) and Danish Hnaef, so that they fell in slaughter in Frisia. While the *shope* sings something like the *Finnsburg Fragment*, the poet meditates upon the tragedy resulting from that well-known fight. The *shope's* preoccupations are heroic, as is appropriate; the poet's are humane. "He dwells on the pathetic situation of Queen Hildeburh and on the spiritual conflict of Hengest" (Bonjour, *Digressions*, p. 58).

1071–72 This is negative understatement. Indeed, Hildeburh had great reason to curse the troth-breaking Jutes (or "enemies"), if they were responsible for the deaths of her son and her brother. Kaske makes a good argument for translating the word *eotenas* in this passage "giants" as elsewhere in the poem, meaning here "enemies." I offer my reason for retaining the usual translation "Jutes" in the note on line 1141.

1080–85 On the morning after the fight ends (it went on for five days, according to the *Finnsburg Fragment*, but this may be poetic exaggeration) Finn finds that he has too few men to drive Hengest from the hall he occupies. Hengest, on the other hand, does not have enough men to break out from the hall successfully. A treaty seems the only solution, though there is a loss of honor for all concerned.

1102 "Making peace with the slayers of one's lord was entirely contrary to the Germanic code of honor." (Klaeber)

1117–18 It would appear to be Hildeburh who is singing. It is customary for a woman to sing at the funeral pyre, perhaps for the purpose of calling down good spirits to help the soul of the departed warrior in his journey "elsewhere." See the note on lines 3150–55 below.

1118 "The warrior ascended": It seems to me that Grimm's suggestion, "The warrior's spirit rose into the air," is by far the best of the many explanations proposed. Others explain that Hnaef is here being lifted onto the pyre.

1129 "He cast no lots" to prepare for an ocean-going venture by reading the omens. I translate *unhlitme* thus because I believe that such divination was a standard practice in the seafaring culture of the ancient north.

1141 The Jutes are, according to Klaeber, Frisians under King Finn (Klaeber, p. 232). They are mentioned four times, at lines 1072, 1088, 1141 and 1145, but never do I find that they are clearly aligned with one side or another; one can construct an argument either way. As there is a tradition that a mercenary warrior Hengist (a Jute) was hired at about this time by a Celtic king, Vortigern, to come to fight for him in Britain, and this Hengist also turned out to be an oath breaker (though without the excuse of vengeance for a beloved lord), I like to think that the two are the same, that Hnaef's warrior Hengest fulfilled his duty toward his dead lord by avenging his slaying, but could not then return to Denmark because he or his Jutish comrades (or his Jutish foes of family feud, serving King Finn) had instigated the fight in the first place (lines 1071–72), on what was intended to be a peaceful visit. Therefore, when the Danes took home the queen and the plunder, the Jutes who had been their companions turned their sights toward that "green and pleasant land" across the sea, and spearheaded the invasion of Angles, Saxons, and Jutes that eventually changed the name of that land to Engleland. This is pure conjecture; there is no way of proving it. But an alternative translation for *he Eotena bearn* in line 1141 is "he, a man of the Jutes"; the translation as I have rendered it accords with Klaeber's interpretation that the Jutes are fighting on the side of the Frisians and that Hengest is a Dane, but either rendering is grammatically valid.

1143–44 Some have suggested that *him . . . on bearm dyde* means that the sword was plunged into Hengest's breast. But *Cotton Maxims II* (25–26) makes it clear that, just as the spear shall be in the hand, the gem on the ring, the mast on the ship, and the dragon in the barrow, so the proper place for the sword is ready in the lap: *Sweord sceal on bearme, drihtlic isern*. To the sword name (or kenning) "Light of Battle" compare the evocative use of such sword-light as an opening for the *Finnsburg Fragment* and later in this poem: "Sword-light flashed/as though all Finnsburg were on fire!" (See also the speculations below on line 1570.)

1148 Guthlaf and Oslaf are probably identical to Guthlaf and Ordlaf in the *Fragment*, line 14.

1149 This is probably the journey made to Frisia the year before. Guthlaf and Oslaf are complaining a great deal about the sudden attack after the sea journey.

1164–68 "Still" suggests some event to follow that will contradict this scene, and may be a hint about Hrothulf's disloyalty (for a forceful argument against this proposal, see Kenneth Sisam, *The Structure of Beowulf*). Unferth, sitting at their feet, here seems to me to function almost as a symbol of faithlessness between kin. "They trusted his *ferhðe* "courage," even though the very name Unferth should serve as a warning. (Further hints of disaster occur at *Beowulf* 82–85 and *Widsith* 45–46; in this latter poem we are told that "Hrothulf and Hrothgar held peace together for a very long time.")

1175–87 The standard interpretation of Wealtheow's speech is that it is an ironic fore-shadowing of the disaster that is to befall her sons. But is it not possible that Wealtheow, whose duty as queen is to keep peace between kinsmen and arouse warriors to their proper tasks, comprehends the danger of the situation: young sons, an old king, and a powerful nephew of the king? Some have said that she is worried lest Hrothgar should plan to leave part of his kingdom to Beowulf, whom he has "adopted." I believe that Wealtheow recognizes this adoption as a ceremonial to do Beowulf honor (it is accompanied with lavish treasures), and that she is taking the opportunity suggested by this adoption, perhaps reinforced by the idea of peace-weaving gone wrong in the lay about Finnsburg, to suggest to Hrothgar that he should make a firm provision to leave the kingdom to a strong kinsman, like Hrothulf, whom she believes will be kind to her boys (it is impossible to be sure whether the poet's tone here is ironic or not), in order to prevent tragedy before it has the opportunity to arise. This is the line taken by Hygd later in the poem when she offers the rule of the Geatish kingdom to Beowulf over her own son's head (lines 2369–76).

1197–1201   Hama is apparently an adventurer who robbed Eormenric, a king of the East Goths who died by his own hand around 375 A.D., of the precious *Brosinga mene*, possibly identical to the *Brisinga men*, the magical necklace of Freya in Old Norse legend. In *Thidrek's Saga* it is told that a certain Heimir fled the enmity of Erminrikr and later entered a monastery, bringing with him all his treasures. Possibly "eternal gain" implies that Hama entered a monastery, choosing eternal over secular wealth, and the monastery may be the "bright city" to which he carried the Brosinga mene.

1202–14   This is the first of the allusions to Hygelac's Frisian expedition, an ill-judged raid on which he lost his life. At 2172 Beowulf gives the necklace to Hygelac's queen Hygd; she may have given it to Hygelac to wear for luck on this particular raid.

1214   *Heal swege onfeng*, which I have understood as "the hall received the sound" and paraphrased "applause had greeted . . . ," has been amended by some editors to *heals-bege onfeng* "he (Beowulf) accepted the necklace." This makes good sense, but I believe that, as in the case of the Finnsburg digression, the poet has been meditating on the history behind a lay being sung by the *shope*; in this case the lay is an "appropriate" story to accompany the giving of a priceless necklace, the story of the Brosinga mene. After the song is over, there is applause: *heal swege onfeng.*

1239–40   The hall is being cleared of tables, which are lifted from their trestles and hung on the wall. It is then *brǣded* throughout with beds and pillows. These are laid directly on the broad benches on which the warriors will sleep. The "beds" (or "feather-beds") are probably soft eiderdowns, like thick sleeping bags or quilts; we still use such old-fashioned mattresses in my home in Yorkshire. The verb *bregdan* (past participle *brǣded*), used for a quick action like the drawing of a sword, suggests the fluffing up of the feather-beds that is necessary before they can be slept on comfortably.

1261–66   The Cain theme is recapitulated, and in 1266–76 the Grendel story is summarized, almost as though the story had been broken off and were being continued at a different time. The same kind of summarizing of what has gone before occurs following line 2000, when Beowulf reports on the events in Denmark to his lord, Hygelac. It has been suggested that *Beowulf* was designed to be presented before an audience as a three-part sequence.

1262   Cain uses a sword rather than the more traditional jawbone of an ass both in the poem and in certain medieval illustrations of this episode from Genesis.

1331   In view of the fact that Grendel's tracks had been followed to the mere the morning after he was defeated in Heorot (837–852), it is inconsistent that the poet should have Hrothgar "know not whither" Grendel's mother carried her grisly load. A recent commentator has suggested retaining the manuscript reading and translating "I know not *whether* . . . " that is, whether Grendel's mother bore the corpse away at all, or ate it on the spot. I prefer to read the emended "whither," believing that as is frequently the case, the poet is more interested in the suggestive mood he is creating than in the consistency of his story: Grendel's lake is a weird, shadowy, *imprecise* place.

1345–76   The description of the monsters' dwelling place is a kind of set piece, one of the most famous passages of the poem, and perhaps the poet's justified eagerness to include it helps to account for Hrothgar's inconsistent ignorance. Three apparently conflicting analogies for this passage have been pointed out by scholars, with the purpose of explaining particlar details:

1. Lawrence showed, with references to the *Grettissaga*, that the scene seems to be a waterfall with a pool before it and a cave behind it; if this is taken strictly, then the sea monsters are yet another inconsistency. Yet of course one then immediately thinks of landlocked Loch Ness and the first written reference to the monster there that is almost contemporary with *Beowulf*, and of the pictures of monsters goggling at the rudders of ships on the Götland stones.

2. There seems to be an allusion here to the Christian Hell; the burning lake, the bottomless deep, the *wyrmas*, and the misty wasteland all are echoes of other early accounts of Hell both in Latin and in Old English literature. There are especially close parallels to the seventeenth Blickling Homily, which is based on a Visio Pauli, about the wanderings of Paul in the desert.

3. There seem to be classical echoes as well. "In fact," Klaeber says, "those passages which we are tempted to regard as 'Vergilian' are especially striking in this section."

The landscape of the mere, then, seems to be intended as an allusive series of montage effects culminating in a suitable lair for monsters, rather than as a place one could plot on a map. (Nevertheless, each time I read about it, I see an exaggerated version of the landscape I live in myself, the bleak moors, the cavernous mountain Ingleborough, and the tarns of the high fells in my area of the Yorkshire Dales. There is even a Grendel figure, Yordas the giant, who dwells in a local waterfall cave and is said to eat little boys, and up near Black Shiver Moss is a sinister shake-hole called "Batty Wife Hole.")

1570   *Lixte se leoma* is usually taken to refer to the firelight mentioned in line 1516, and so I have translated it "the flame leapt up." Yet Beowulf has just cut off the head of Grendel's mother and her blood is running down the sword. Presumably her blood is hot like that of her son (1616) and of Sigemund's dragon (897). Can it be the sword, then, that is called a *leoma* "flame" like the sword *beadoleoma* of 1523, lighting up the hall? The golden banner in the dragon's lair pours forth light by which Wiglaf can see the treasures (2769–71). The sword that gleams in the presence of the enemy is a standard folklore motif (familiar to readers of Tolkien), and may account for the "burning" at the beginning of the *Finnsburg Fragment* and the flashing light of battle later in that poem.

1588–90   Klaeber says, "To an unprejudiced reader it may seem natural enough that the head of Grendel, the chief of the enemies, is cut off and carried home in triumph. But, as an additional reason, the desire of preventing the ghost from haunting Heorot has been cited." (In Scandinavian fairy tales a troll must be beheaded in order to destroy it completely.) A further reason for the beheading may stem originally from Celtic sources, like the Norse myth of Mimur's head kept by Odin to foretell the future. It was an early Celtic custom to preserve the articulate dead heads of powerful friends and enemies for this purpose, or simply for "luck"—a more tangible quality then than now.

1605–11   The sword melts like an icicle, and the powerful metaphor leads into an image of God the Father "unwinding the water ropes" of ice in the springtime. This is in some sense analogous to Beowulf's "cleansing" of the waters of the lake (1620).

1652   The culture hero returns from the underworld with shamanistic "sea treasures," as do Gilgamesh and Aeneas. The magical hilt is proof of his power which the king will adopt as a focus for prophetic wisdom. Such magical treasures, having the power of breaking a paralysis which holds warriors in thrall, appear even in Joyce's *Ulysses*, where Stephen's sword-like ashplant and Bloom's moly-like potato free them from the Circean Nighttown and aid them with the wisdom to progress past their stultifying fantasies.

1667   The melting blade picks up the candle and icicle motifs of 1570–72 and 1605–08.

1669–70   Beowulf's code and vocation are implicit in his announcement that he avenged "wicked deeds, the deaths of the Danes," as was proper. His narrow (and natural) view of the feud, thinking that it is now over, is corrected by Hrothgar's broader vision in his "sermon."

1677–99   The hilt is described. Before speaking, Hrothgar "looked on the hilt," and it focuses his royal, hence more than human, wisdom, much as the sacred pagan well in Carlisle apparently focused the second sight of St. Cuthbert (Bede, *Life of St. Cuthbert*, 27). Just as enemy heads aided the prophecies of Irish warriors in ancient sagas (or even uttered the prophecies), and certain sacred pools of water aided in the wisdom of Celtic and English saints, so in ancient Rome a lamp with shaded flame was sometimes used (this may have been in Paul's mind when he said that we see now as through glass, darkly). Christians traditionally focus their meditation upon a cross, hoping either for supernatural inspiration or more simply the stillness of mind which begets wisdom; the crossed hilt of a sword has been known to serve the same purpose.

The text tells us that two things are "written" on the hilt: the beginning of the ancient fight (which is given a setting *for us alone* in the context of scriptural history in lines 1689–93) and the name of the first owner, in runes. A combination of runic and nonrunic inscriptions is not uncommon; technically Hrothgar should be able to read runes. But we are not told that he reads what he is looking at, and even if he did, the scriptural history, whether in runes, Roman letters, or pictures, would be unintelligible to him without a context for it: he doesn't know scriptural history. Like any sacral focus for meditation, the object is primarily an aid for gathering one's wits, not intended for discursive understanding about the object itself. Nevertheless, Hrothgar's subsequent homily on the recurrent inward feud of mankind's enemy suggests that he gets the gist at least of the ancient warfare theme inscribed on the hilt. This is the "natural knowledge" of good and evil that Paul says is available to a noble pagan in his letter to the Romans in the New Testament.

1700–84   Hrothgar's advice may be divided into three sections: (1) the exemplum of Heremod, (2) a generalized exposition of the dangers to which the "fortunate man" is exposed, (3) Hrothgar's personal experience. Each section concludes with direct address to Beowulf. (The line division is 1700–24a, 1724b–68, 1769–84.)

1702   Hrothgar as *ethelweard* "guardian of the native land" is a guardian in the ritual sense quite as much as in the sense of war lord. He is the gold giver (and thereby the binder of the community), the keeper of customs, the judge, and here the priest. The same epithet is applied to Beowulf at line 2209.

1705–07   These are expanded lines, containing more than four beats in the Old English; such lines are often reserved for formal statements of great significance, as here. Hrothgar's advice concerns how that dangerous commodity, "fame," must be mediated through wisdom, since Beowulf is to become "an abiding comfort" to his people. Hrothgar's friendship (1707) is expressed with the gift of regal advice as well as treasure.

1719   An essential manifestation of Heremod's evil character was that he "gave no rings" to honor the Danes. Hence he did not fulfill the function of the king as a focuser of human worth, binding the community in a radiating net of aspiration and achievement. His slaughter of comrades at the banquet table is almost a corollary of his niggardliness about rings: he does not value his men.

1831   "The author is inconsistent in representing Hygelac here as still young (see 1968), whereas several years before he had given his daughter in marriage to Eofor (2997–98)"—Klaeber.

1931–62   This sudden introduction of a character from right outside the story has evoked a great deal of critical discussion but, as Irving remarks repeatedly in his *A Reading of Beowulf*, the poet has a habit of describing persons in terms of what they are not: Hygd is not like Thryth. He also takes great pleasure in high contrast, like juxtaposing nobel Sigemund and ignoble Heremod. It seems to me that there is a strong parallel between the "evil shadow" figures Heremod and Thryth: both were miserly and both slaughtered their friends. Hygd, like Wealtheow, is the epitome of a peace-weaver, known for her generosity and for "loving her people" (1982). The significance of the story of Thryth (as of Heremod) would seem to be that as you cease to honor your people with rings, you may turn to slaying them. Thryth has fallen into this neurotic position, and it is only her marriage with the hero Offa that saves her.

Offa, who is referred to in sources other than *Beowulf*, is thought to have lived in the second half of the fourth century, and is known primarily for a heroic fight mentioned in *Widsith* (35–44). Klaeber, after a long exposition of sources and stories concerning both the fourth century Offa of continental Anglia and his descendent Offa II of Mercia in England (roughly contemporary with the composition of *Beowulf*), concludes only that "the poet was interested in the old Anglian traditions . . . that are concerned with persons belonging to English (i.e., pre-English) stock."

1936–38   The manner in which Thryth's victims are slain, first having a rope twisted around their necks to strangle them, then being pierced by a blade to finish them off, corresponds exactly to the description of ritual slaughter by the Arab Ibn Fadlan in his *risala*, when he

observed such rituals among the Scandinavian Rus in the mid-tenth century. A similar ritual slaughter is depicted upon the Franks Casket as I interpret it (see my article concerning the right side of the casket in *Neuphilologus Mitteilungen*, 73 (1972), 30–34, where further references may be found).

1969   The text describes Hygelac as "Ongentheow's slayer," but only by proxy did he kill the Swedish king; later (2484–90) it is made clearer that Hygelac wreaked vengeance upon his brother's slayer through the hand of Eofor. I have taken the liberty, here as elsewhere, of spelling things out, paraphrasing "Ongentheow's slayer" as "Hygelac . . . who had ordered the slaying of Ongentheow."

2000–2162   Beowulf's report to his king about the events in Denmark not only sums up what happened there but shifts the focus: the monsters become more folkloristic and the political situation becomes more real. Details are added, like the name of the slain Geat Hondshio and the "glove" carried by Grendel, which makes him more troll-like than ever; and one sees Beowulf's political acuity as he sets Freawaru's graciousness against the feuds surrounding her marriage to Ingeld the Heathobard, and offers no optimism about how the tense situation will be resolved.

2024–69   The story of Ingeld's revenge for the slaying of his father Froda is told by Saxo Grammaticus with slight changes: Klaeber gives a full summary of Saxo's account.

2039–2143   This long section comprises both fits 29 and 30. I have titled the whole "The Fated Hall" as it contains, first, Beowulf's anticipation of the way the Danish-Heathobard feud will break out again, a feud that will lead to a battle in Heorot (See *Widsith*, 45–49), and presumably to the burning of the hall alluded to in *Beowulf* 82–85, and, second, his abbreviated account of the two monster fights (2069–2143). I have divided the feuds part of the section from the monster part with a picture in the text.

2152   Editors vary on interpreting the Old English compound as "boar head-sign" or "boar-head sign," the latter denoting a banner with the figure of a boar's head on it. Since elsewhere in the poem the images of boars are associated with helmets, I have chosen the first interpretation; it corresponds to the ritual helmets crested with boars in the Swedish helmet plates from Torslunda (see the illustration in fit 19) and an actual such boar crest found at Benty Grange in England.

2195   A hide of land has been described as the amount of land required to maintain one free household, or the amount that may be plowed by an ox in a year. The actual acreage varies greatly according to place and period. In his *History* (III, 24), Bede mentions that the size of North Mercia is seven thousand hides, the same land measure that the poet gives us for Beowulf's estate.

2200   It is here that Klaeber breaks the poem, marking this as the beginning of Part II and noting that what folows is "much broken up by digressions." As I have put the digressions in italics, the last third of the poem may be read either as a relatively fast narrative about the dragon and the death of Beowulf, or more slowly and with fuller significance as an interweaving of human strife having discernible historical causes and nonhuman disaster which strikes when all seems peaceful and men least expect it.

2211–31   Much of the text here is illegible in the manuscript, and has been reconstructed by the editors.

2223   Old English *þeow* "servant" is a reconstruction based upon all that remains visible of this word, only the first letter, thorn (th). Other possible reconstructions are *þeof* "thief" and *þegn* "thane."

2228–31   The text is still very uncertain here, but what seems indisputable, especially when supported by later passages, is that a cup was stolen from the dragon's hoard, and this theft was taken by the dragon as an overt action demanding vengeance.

2231–81   The history of the hoard in these lines is dominated by the "Lay of the Last Survivor" (lines 2233–70), a passage which, like the description of Grendelsmere and the later "Father's Lament," has occasionally been abstracted from its context to stand alone as evocative poetry. Though it may be thus abstracted, its link with the rest of the poem is seen by Bonjour to go beyond the setting of mood and the establishing of the history of the hoard: "The story of the destruction of a people and the lament of the wretched man who survived the catastrophe foreshadow the very situation in store for the Geats after Beowulf's death" (*Digressions*, p. 69). What follows the lament, the information about the nature of dragons, is found also in *Cotton Maxims II* (see the note to line 887): it is the nature of a dragon to seek out buried gold and to guard it. The juxtaposition of these two passages, about the burial of the gold and the dragon, has led some to suggest, most recently G. V. Smithers and Jorge Luis Borges, that, like Fafnir of the Sigurd story, the last survivor himself turned into the dragon to guard the gold. This is not what the poem says.

2287 Klaeber says, "Probably not 'strife was renewed,' but (lit.) 'strife arose which previously did not exist.' " In context of the Great Feud, established for us the audience and related to scriptural history in the first part of the poem, the dragon is not simply a creature coming out from the existential darkness to strike at the fellowship of men, but an envoy of evil. In this sense, recurrent strife against mankind is indeed "renewed."

2329–31 Some recent commentators would capitalize Ancient Law and Beowulf's fleeting perception here may well be related to his natural knowledge of good and evil. But these verses need not be understood in terms of such a Christian perspective from Beowulf's point of view; he is king, the guardian of the gift throne that has been burnt, and it is a perfectly natural mythic response to feel that the disaster may have been directed against him personally, and to cast around for what he has done to deserve it "as was not his custom." Margaret Goldsmith assumes that if Beowulf felt such pangs, then he was indeed guilty of some spiritual crime (which she identifies as avarice).

2333–36 Miss Goldsmith doubts the virtue of Beowulf's motives, but here the poet makes those motives entirely clear: the dragon burnt down the Weathermark hall, destroying the gift-throne and the security of the Geats, and "for that" the king planned to seek revenge. It was his duty as *ethelweard* "protector of the native land." The gaining of the dragon's gold, a secondary motive of the fight, could be interpreted as seeking a compensation for the destruction of the kingdom's treasure. Just as it honors a slain kinsman to obtain *wergild* "man gold" for him, so it both will retrieve the honor and strengthen the kingdom of the Geats to obtain "ethelgild" (my word) for the gift-throne, the heart of the kingdom, that has been destroyed.

2361 Klaeber's note suggests that Beowulf is carrying "thirty sets of armor" with him while swimming. This is hard to imagine; even if he has the strength of thirty men in his arm, the awkward picture presented by this interpretation is grotesque. Hence I have translated *hildegeatwa* "war-equipments" as "trophies," with the implication that he has taken a helmet here and a sword there, but not the complete gear of all thirty of the enemies he has slain. Even so it is hard to conceive, and Fred C. Robinson offers an ingenious alternative solution, that the poet does not specify quantity, and that the number thirty found at the text in this place, in Roman numerals, is possibly the displaced missing fit number XXX (see the note on lines 2039–2143 above).

2428–29 It was one method of securing peace between tribes or households to place a child in the care of others for his education. Bede was placed in a monastery at the age of seven (*History*, V, 24). In Germanic societies a noble man was often responsible for the training of his "sister's son," and bore a special relationship to him, as Sigemund did to Fitela (see 875–889). This explains why it was so particularly distressing to Hildeburh to see her son and her brother dead as enemies on the battlefield, and she lays them together on the funeral pyre in the relationship that they should have borne in life. It was an essential function of the peace-weaving practice whereby a king would give his daughter in marriage to the son of a foreign household (as Hrothgar planned to give Freawaru to Ingeld of the Heathobards) that the child of that union would then return to the mother's native home, where her brother would assume a sort of "godfather" role for him, thus intensifying the kinship bond between tribes. Beowulf is "sister's son" to Hygelac, and gives that relationship all the respect demanded of him by his culture.

2434–43 When a Germanic warrior was murdered, it was important both to his spirit in the afterlife and to the peace of mind of his kinsfolk that honor should be done him by offering *wergild* (man gold), just as it is important in a Christian society that the dead should receive proper formal blessing. Because Herebald's death is an accident, no redress, either in punishment of the slayer or in *wergild*, can be taken; the death is literally "unaccountable." His inability to resolve his dear son's death causes Hrethel to fall ill (an illness to which today we

might give a psychological name); with this grief upon him, he dies (lines 2462–71).

2444–62 This passage, called "The Father's Lament," is the only extended simile (or comparison) in the poem of the kind familiar in Homeric epic and used by Milton. It is offered by Beowulf as an analogy to the helplessness felt by Hrethel when his son dies in circumstances unsuitable for vengeance. The prominence given to *wyrd* in that accidental slaying and "the poignant atmosphere of grief and sadness" in "The Father's Lament" together "prepare the central theme and dominant mood of the end of the poem" (Bonjour, *Digressions*, p. 34).

2456–57 The manuscript text of 2456 and my interpretation of the words *reote* "round-harp" and *ridend* "rhythms" in 2457 differ from Klaeber's interpretation, "the wind-swept resting place deprived of joy" where "riders sleep." The chief improvement in my reading is grammatical concord between noun and verb in 2457b, and a clarification of its relationship to 2458a. (Though I use the word "round-harp" in my translation, I have argued in my article on these lines that the poet is actually using a technical term for an instrument more like a harp-zither, a rotta; as this word is like the name of a later English instrument which is quite different, I have suppressed it in favor of the more usual hall instrument.)

2501 By slaying Dayraven, Beowulf avenged Hygelac's death in battle on the ill-advised Frisian expedition. Such vengeance was the duty of a loyal follower, and to be expected, but Beowulf's description suggests the novelty of taking vengeance bare-handed. Klaeber notes that Dayraven (*Daeghrefn*) is a Frankish, non-Anglo-Saxon name.

Sources outside *Beowulf* help to clarify the tangle of tribes and names attached to this expedition, which seems to have actually taken place early in the fifth century. Hygelac sailed through Frisian waters to land and ravage on Hetware shores, but then made the mistake of letting the main part of his fleet sail for home with the booty. With his remaining small force he was overtaken by Theodebert, the son of the Frankish king Theoderic (the Merovingian of line 2921), who defeated him with a much larger force, and in that defeat he was slain. Hygelac's enemies in that final battle appear to be Frisians, Hetwares, and Franks, united in a single force under the Merovingian ruler.

2538–2711 Klaeber notes three distinct phases in the dragon fight, just as there were three phases in the fight with Grendel's mother. In the first phase (2538–91) Beowulf fights alone and damages his sword; in the second (2592–2687) Wiglaf intervenes; and in the third (2688–2711) the two kinsmen succeed in slaying the dragon.

2600–01 Such truisms as this offer us an insight into the preoccupations of Germanic society. Here it is offered as a contrast to the attitude of the battle shirkers as they flee, and at the same time as a keynote for what will follow, summarizing the motivation of Wiglaf, who stands for the highest ideal of the thane in his tribal society.

2611–25 The digression on the sword which Wiglaf brandishes so bravely in his lord's defense suggests a future scene in the land of the Geats rather like the Heathobard invasion of Heorot. With the defender of the kingdom dead, the Swedish king will not long stand for the ignominy of a slain kinsman's weapon being borne by a Geatish son of the slayer.

It has been suggested that Weohstan, Wiglaf's father, is the Wehha of the East Anglian genealogies, and that Wiglaf himself may have taken what remained of the Geats to England after the loss of their greatest warriors, their king, and their treasure, in order to try to preserve their clan as a separate entity unendangered by Swedish invasion. Such a speculation does suggest a solution to the problem of how the armor of a Swedish warrior happened to be among the equipment buried in the East Anglian cenotaph at Sutton Hoo in England.

2697–99 As Klaeber notes, this passage may be interpreted in either of two ways. Does "he did not heed the dragon's head" mean that he paid no attention to the flames the beast was spewing and plunged his sword hand in anyway, or that he did not aim for the head but had the good sense to strike lower?

Margaret Goldsmith's comments on "heeding the head" are of interest. She quotes Gregory and Augustine on Genesis 3:15 *observabit caput*, which both writers take "as an injunction to be vigilant against the Devil's *suggestio*" (p. 233). In any case, "right thinking" is stressed throughout the fight (see the note below). It is up to the reader whether this is to be interpreted as the common sense needed to fight dragons or as moral vigilance.

2703 *geweold his gewitte*, which I have translated "came to his senses," marks a sub-theme of the dragon fight. As Irving says, in this part of the poem Wiglaf stands out against those whose "refusal to act has meant the obliteration of their heroic identity" (p. 169). Yet not only is the need to act stressed, and in particular the need to act as sibb-athelings (lines 2600–01 state this theme), but also the need to act wittingly, in contrast to performing mere intoxicated valor.

2705 Dragons are vulnerable only in their stomachs, just as trolls can only be destroyed by cutting off their heads. When Beowulf comes to his senses and ceases flailing about with his useless sword, he goes to work like a butcher, "writing off" the worm with a single clean knife-thrust into what he well knows to be the dragon's vital spot.

2715–19 Compare *The Wanderer*, lines 88–89:

> Who then thinks wisely about this wall-place
> and deeply ponders this dark life . . .

Likewise in *The Ruin* ancient walls bring reflections about life and death. As Beowulf looks at the securely built barrow (described in terms which are touched with allegory), he meditates upon the passing of his days and speaks of kinship and the deeds he has done in the world. This sequence of object regarded, meditation, and formal speech seems to be an Anglo-Saxon poetic convention particularly in connection with ancient walls.

2717 Klaeber quotes a passage from Saxo Grammaticus in which that historian wonders whether giants could be responsible for the megalithic tombs of his country; here as elsewhere "giants" are understood to be members of a race inhabiting the land in the past (the Romans in England are sometimes referred to as "giants" in connection with their ruins). No one who has been in the presence of a megalithic monument will find the idea of giants wholly absurd.

2741–42 As mentioned above (note to 913–915), much of the characterization of Beowulf is in terms of what he is not. Here a theme built up throughout the poem (with some suspense, in Hrothgar's cautionary sermon) is resolved: In his treatment of his kinsmen, Beowulf is utterly unlike Cain, Unferth, Heremod, Hnaef, Thryth, Hathcyn, and, in a sense, Onla.

2756 The dragon's cave is described in terms which simultaneously suggest a hall with benches along the wall and a large stone grave covered with a mound, typical of northern Europe.

2766 Both *oferhigian*, which I translate "overpower," and *hyde*, which I translate "heed," have been variously interpreted. *Oferhygian* has been compared with modern dialect *over-hye*, "to over-reach, overtake," and with *ofer-hyd*, *oferhydig* "proud." *Hyde*, according to some, means *hede*, "heed," according to others means "hide." Both *hydan* and *hedan* have been used before in the poem in connection with heads (446 and 2697), and here the two senses of these verbs seem to be blended, to suggest (partly through the association of the two alliterating syllables, *hig* and *hyd*, with *hygd*, *gehygd* "thought") that whoever may hide the gold, it will overpower the mind of every man, no matter who attempts to beware of that event. G. V. Smithers suggests that this is an example of the poet's distrust of gold, but the distrust is entirely consistent with the view expressed later (3069–75 and 3167–68) about gold *in the ground*. It is hoarded gold, gold that is no longer serving the social function of binding men together through its use as a token of worth, that isolates men, giving them wolfish thoughts and making them dragonish. Much of the poet's preoccupation throughout this section of the poem seems to be a concern about self-seeking individualism as opposed to a commitment to the group.

2769 The banner glows like Grendel's eyes and (possibly) the bloodied sword in Grendelsmere. A standard, perhaps for a banner, was found in the Sutton Hoo ship-burial, and one is mentioned in Shield's ship-burial, where it is carefully placed at that warrior's head. That in the Sutton Hoo cenotaph was placed, in relation to the armor and weapons, above where the head would have been had a body been there.

2799 Manuscript *minne* was first emended by Ettmüller to *mine* "my," to make it agree with *feorhlege* "life," and this has been accepted by editors since. But in view of Beowulf's lament that he has no *yrfeweard* (2731)(which Klaeber glosses "heir" but which means "guardian of *yrfe*"), and if *yrfe* is to be taken as cognate with Old Norse *erfi* "grave-ale," perhaps there is meant to be suggested in manuscript *minne* something like Old Norse *minni* "drink in loving memory," and this emendation is ill-advised. Perhaps the unemended text of this line should be translated, "I have sold *minni* for a hoard of treasure" in comparison with *Christ and Satan* 577: "He sold the Son of God for a treasure of silver." If the line means something like this,

then the act represents an extraordinary sacrifice on Beowulf's part, since he would believe that *minni* "loving remembrance," like *lof* "esteem, glory," assures the recipient of a kind of pagan immortality. Another possibility is that *minne* is the masculine accusative pronoun meaning "what is mine," that is, his life. In either case he is giving up what is most important to him in exchange for the gold that he thinks will aid his people. This reading is in direct contradiction to Margaret Goldsmith's. She claims that lines 2749–2800 "emphasize the poverty of Beowulf's barter, his life the price of a mouldering hoard which brings no good to anyone in the story. This is the very antithesis of the Christian exchange of worldly wealth for everlasting life" (*The Mode and Meaning of Beowulf*, p. 239). What she overlooks is the fact that the principle she cites is individual and spiritual, whereas Beowulf's function in the poem is almost wholly social and secular.

2800 This is usually interpreted as a direct command to Wiglaf: "Watch over my people." But it seems to me likely that Beowulf is saying that the treasures will take care of the needs of his people, now that he may not remain among them, and that the verb is in the present third person plural with future meaning.

2802 Editors recognize a Homeric parallel in Beowulf's description of the barrow he wants his people to build for him. Wrenn quotes the *Odyssey* (24): "Then around them [the bones of Achilles] did we, the holy host of Argive warriors, pile a great and glorious tomb, on a jutting headland above the broad Hellespont, that it might be seen afar from off the sea by men, both by those who now are, and by those who shall be hereafter." Klaeber cites other parallels in classical literature, but none are so close in manner of expression. The rites of Odin in the *Ynglinga Saga* are similar.

2814 Klaeber emends manuscript *forspeof* to *forsweop* "swept off" on the basis of line 477; Wrenn, however, argues convincingly for a more conservative reading *forspeon*, which he translates "lured away." One is tempted to think of the classical concept of the Fates spinning out the lives of the warriors to their "measured end" and of the women who weave war-luck in *Njal's Saga* (see the note to line 697). The reading *forspeon* ("spun out completely"?) could bear such a construction.

2819–20 This passage marks a real point of suspense in the poem in the context of the Father/fire alternatives for life after death given in lines 185–188. "The judgment of the just" is ambiguous, and can refer either to the judgment accorded to righteous pagans (the secular glory that will live after them) or to the judgment given by the Righteous, in a Christian sense. (It is in this sense, of course, that Margaret Goldsmith takes it, pp. 178–179, in her argument that Beowulf is condemned.)

2891 Tacitus (*Germania*, 6) says that among the Germanic tribes suicide was the last refuge from disgrace (much as falling on one's sword was the Roman response to a humiliating defeat).

2911–12 and following. The prediction of trouble at the death of a powerful king is a standard feature both of epic poetry and of tribal encomium. In this case the poet has built up the atmosphere of feuds surrounding the Geats so forcefully that it seems probable that the prediction is no mere rhetorical gesture, but will come true. Some Swedish historians like to think that the fall of the kingdom to the Swedes after Beowulf's death was a historical event marking the foundation of the Swedish kingdom as a political entity, and establishing that kingdom as the oldest continuous political state in Europe.

2922–98 Klaeber points out that this battle in Ravenswood is the only detailed account of a real battle in *Beowulf*. He calls attention to Saxo's account of the slaying of Athislus (Eadgils) and its similar details.

3014 Here it is said that the dragon's treasures must be burnt on the pyre, but later (3163–68) the poet tells us that they were buried in the new mound.

3026–27 The wolf and birds of prey as "beasts of battle" are a standard motif of heroic poetry, but in *Beowulf* the poet has withheld use of the combination until this point, when it is presented most evocatively, and not heroically at all, as the climax of a prophecy of doom. (For the general tone of lines 3018–27 compare the lament of the last survivor, 2262–66.)

3049 Klaeber suggests that the treasure has lain buried in the place chosen by the last survivor for three hundred years (2278), but that it was possibly buried elsewhere before that.

An alternative explanation of this discrepancy could be that the treasure was buried a thousand years ago, but the dragon has only been guarding it for the last three hundred. I suspect, however, that in relating mythical events of prehistory, the poet used both three hundred years and a thousand to represent "a long time," without the intention of being specific.

3051–57 and 3069–75 The curse laid by "those long-ago princes" upon the "heathen treasure" (2216) has evoked much comment. But surely the poet's own comment that God would allow the appropriate man to open that hoard, and Beowulf's avowed purpose in obtaining it for his people (2794–2800), not to feed his own greed, suggests that, although he met his death in the dragon fight, the part of the curse that mentions idol-worship was not applicable to him. Believing that the poet at all times regards Beowulf as a noble pagan, doing the best he can within his limited sphere of spiritual understanding, I have translated the great crux of lines 3074–75 accordingly. These two lines and 2819–20 give us our only clues concerning the state of Beowulf's soul at death, and the poet has made it clear at the beginning of his poem that this is a crucial matter (183–188). My solution leaves unsolved only the problem of the concord of *goldhwæte* (which I translate "greedy for gold"). Klaeber emends the text and translates, "unless God's grace had before more readily favored those eager for gold," which I do not find a happy solution. Nor do I believe with Margaret Goldsmith that these two lines tell us that Beowulf was damned.

3077–78 Most have taken Wiglaf's remark about "the will of one man" as critical of Beowulf's heroic stance and a reflection of the poet's view. Garmonsway has suggested that it represents Wiglaf's failure to perceive the transcendent standard of conduct by which Beowulf acted, yet Wiglaf recognizes Beowulf as a hero of high destiny only a few lines on (3084). To me the speech seems to carry the ambivalence expressed by the speaker of *Wulf and Eadwacer*, "It was joyful to me, yet hateful also."

3137–82 We have three accounts of funeral obsequies in *Beowulf,* at the beginning, middle, and end of the poem. Shield's funeral contained no burning, only a ship sent out to sea; Hnaef's contained the pyre but no further ceremony; and Beowulf's, grander than either of the others, has both, first the pyre and then the burial, in this case on a mound overlooking the sea rather than a sea-burial, with a goodly display of treasure at each stage. The discovery of the treasure-burial at Sutton Hoo in 1939 aroused particular excitement among *Beowulf* scholars, not only because objects found there were so similar in detail to some of those described in the poem, but also because this "richest of treasures found on English soil" offered an archaeological parallel to the lavishness of Beowulf's burial, which had before been thought merely an indication of the poet's fanciful imagination.

3145 Howell D. Chickering, Jr., on the basis of a reasonable emendation by Sophus Bugge, personifies the flame as a dancer in his translation. In his Commentary he remarks on how fire has been personified earlier in the poem, and he says, "Here it is 'awakened' and then takes its proper place in the ritual as a roaring warrior doing a funeral dance" (p. 377).

3150–55 The text greatly obliterated here, has given rise to much discussion including one full book on these lines alone.

Wrenn believes that the "woman with her hair bound up" must have been Beowulf's widow, but this goes against the feeling of the poem that he is a warrior-king unencumbered with such personal relationships. The figure of such a woman appears in silver and pewter, on tapestries, and specifically in the funeral context on the Götland picture stones contemporary with the poem. In the *risala* of Ibn Fadlan an old woman called the "Angel of Death" presides over the funeral ceremonies of a chieftain who dies while the Arab traveler is sojourning among the Rus. In *Thorfinn's Saga* there is an illuminating parallel to the practice of singing associated with prophecy (though not in the funeral context). A spaewife is preparing for her trance, and says that she needs a woman who can sing the song called *Varthlokur;* a girl is found who knows the song and is persuaded to sing it, though reluctantly because she is "a Christian woman." She sings it well, however, and the priestess thanks her, adding that many spirits have come among them "which before were separate from us and would grant us no obedience, and now many things are evident to me of which I was previously unaware."

But the briefly reported lament in *Beowulf* may not be true prophecy at all; in a heroic society it is often customary to foretell disaster at the death of a great king, both as an expression of his value to his people and of fear about what they may really feel to be the case, now that they are without his protection. Professor Tauno Mustanoja relates the lament to other modern and fictional examples of ritual lamentation in *Neuphilologische Mitteilungen,* 68 (1967), 1–27, and concludes, "It was simply a woman's ritual song of lament, and as such it was an essential traditional feature in the funeral ceremony and had to be included in the description" (p. 27).

3166–68 As gold was the life-blood of ancient Scandinavian society, and its chief worth was to give men honor, it loses all vitality and value when buried; Klaeber quotes *Grettissaga,* 18: "All treasure which is hidden in the earth or buried in a howe is in a wrong place." The loss of the gold so sacrifically won is the final ironic futility of the poem, but at the same time the treasure also is a great gift of love and honor in the face of fate, first from Beowulf to his people, then from the people to their dead king. This double evaluation of the loss of the gold, holding two conflicting elements in balance, is an example of a practice raised to an art by this poet.

3182 The last word in the poem is *lofgeornost,* which I translate "most longing for esteem." In terms of the heroic ethic, when his men apply this word to Beowulf it is with unqualified praise, echoed by the later runic inscription on the Ivla stone that I have chosen to illustrate these lines. Other commentators, however, of such eminence as Professors Tolkien and Robinson, have found the phrase, which may also be translated "eager for glory," ambiguous at best in the context of the Christian perspective of the poem.

The student who wishes to go further into matters of criticism and scholarship not mentioned in these notes may wish to consult Beowulf: a Guide to Study, *a manual prepared for this translation. It may be ordered directly from*

Pentangle Press
10490 Santa Monica Blvd.
Los Angeles, CA 90025